ACKNOWLEDGEMENTS

We wish to express our indebtedness to our former student Miss Mary Kevlin who, in the six months that she spent working as a research assistant on the inquiries reported in this monograph, devoted the most meticulous efforts to the work. Her grasp of all the complexities of the design, and the capacity and judgement which she brought to every detail of its execution, were indispensable elements in the success of the study. We are indebted also to Miss Anne Sharp whose assistance in our preliminary investigations of the topic of occupation grading contributed significantly to the design of the later inquiries. We wish particularly to mention the competence, ingenuity, and complete reliability of our administrative secretary, Mrs. Margaret Bett, who rescued the work from serveral critical situations, ranging from the shut-down of our computer as a consequence of a national power shortage to difficulties in getting material printed. It is largely owing to the very high level of competence that these three brought to the study that we were able to prosecute our inquiries with a minimum of expenditure over the above and basic cost of fieldwork.

The work of this monograph was undertaken to provide means of classifying and grading occupations for use in the Oxford occupational mobility inquiry. We are indebted to our colleagues in that inquiry, Mrs. J. E. Floud, Dr. A. H. Halsey, Mr. J. M. Ridge, Miss P. Thorburn, Mrs. C. Llewellyn, Miss J. A. Barton and Mrs. J. Wurglitz for their encouragement, and for valuable suggestions and help at various stages in the work. We also express our thanks to the Warden and Fellows of Nuffield College who initially financed and continue to give material support to our researches into mobility.

At appropriate points in the volume we acknowledge in detail the contribution of our colleagues Dr. D. Robinson, Dr. W. E. J. McCarthy, Dr. R. Martin, and Dr. N. Ellis, and also that of Mrs. Mary Agar of Mary Agar Field Service Ltd. and Mrs. Joan Macfarlane Smith of the British Market Research Bureau. In addition we would record our appreciation of the work of Professor Graham Kalton of Southampton University in drawing up the sample design described in Appendix C. Mr. Jim Hailstone and the operations staff of the Chilton Atlas Computer Laboratory were most helpful in accommodating the special problems created by the unusual design of our inquiries, requiring as it did extensive computing before the fieldwork could be undertaken. Finally, we extend particular thanks to the students and market research interviewers who carried out the interviewing and undertook the exacting work of matching occupation titles to schedules and coding and checking the data.

The study was financed by the Social Science Research Council.

CONTENTS

LIST OF FIGURES AND TABLES

INTRODUCTION

The diversity of occupational classifications and scales already in use in social research is such that any attempt to add to their number must call for some justification. Different kinds of occupation grading will, of course, always be required for different purposes; but the needless development of new grading systems can serve only to increase confusion, and to diminish comparability, in the interpretation of research findings.

The work on occupation grading reported in this monograph was in fact initiated in order to meet the specific requirements of a particular research project—a large-scale inquiry into occupational mobility in England and Wales in which we are engaged, together with a group of our Oxford colleagues. However, the results of our investigations into occupation grading and the new scale to which they give rise are presented here as being of more general interest. The scale that we have developed will, we believe, be widely applicable in social research. The case for its development—and acceptance—that we wish to suggest is that, for most purposes, it will thus contribute to the production of more orderly and comparable data sets.

Before, however, we embark on our presentation of this case, it may be useful to make explicit a distinction which authors of social and psychological measures, and even writers on the theory of test construction, sometimes blur or ignore: that is, the distinction between the procedures which one carries out in attempts to produce a valid and reliable measuring instrument, and the evidence one is able to bring forward for the degree of validity and reliability that the instrument actually possesses. Constructional procedures have the sort of bearing on the success of a scale that scaffolding has on a building: the scaffolding may contribute to the erection of a sound and imposing structure, but the final judgement of the critical onlooker will be passed on the building when the scaffolding is no longer in view.

In the case of the occupational scale on which we report here, the scaffolding consists of a coding system for occupations, the allocation of coded occupations to categories of occupations, the selection of occupation titles to represent categories, and means devised to obtain popular assessments of the representative titles and to assign numerical values to these assessments. Considerable care has gone into the development and testing of the procedures, and not a few reliability coefficients are reported for the various stages. Nevertheless, however much these steps may in practice have contributed to the attainment of a valid and reliable instrument for the grading of occupations, they are irrelevant to the evaluation of the scale which emerges from the constructional procedures. The coefficients relevant to the scale itself can be derived only from application of the scale to a population. In the case of validity, the appropriate coefficient is that which would be obtained if men in a representative sample of the population were assigned to their positions on our scale, and their scale values were then compared with *direct* popular assessments of their occupations; and in the case of reliability, that which would be obtained by comparing the scale values given to a representative sample of the population at two points in time (due allowance being made for actual changes of occupation in the interval).

In this volume, the primary purpose of which is to describe the scale and its making, no such coefficients can be reported. We hope to be in a position to present them at some later date. However, we are able to report certain indirect measures, emerging as by-products of our method of scale construction, which constitute indirect evidence for the degree of reliability attained.

Finally, though, it should be reaffirmed that in a very real sense no manual presenting a scale of this kind can do more than specify an unambiguous set of *a priori* rules and procedures whose actual validity and reliability in particular applications the user must determine for himself. For example, it would be unreasonable to suppose, without recourse to specific empirical evidence, that validity or reliability coefficients for an occupational scale computed from a random sample of the general population would hold good for the population of, say, a coalmining or shipbuilding community with its own highly distinctive occupational structure. The validity and reliability of any measuring instrument may well vary according to the population to which it is applied.

1. GENERAL PROBLEMS OF
OCCUPATIONAL CLASSIFICATIONS AND SCALES

An appraisal of the problems inherent in occupation grading, and thus of the more basic difficulties encountered in using existing occupational classifications and scales, can usefully be conducted under the conventional headings of (i) validity and (ii) reliability. Such an appraisal forms the contents of this initial chapter. In chapters 2 and 3 we shall then set out, and argue for, the methods of achieving relibility and validity which we have ourselves adopted.

We may introduce our discussion of these topics by distinguishing three possible components of the variance of a measuring instrument or scale M. These are (a) the variance of M which it shares with external or objective characteristic X, which is the characteristic that M is supposed to measure; (b) the variance of M which it shares with other objective characteristics Y, Z etc.; and (c) the variance of M which is a result of random processes and which, therefore, is not shared or correlated with any characteristic. Component (a) is the valid variance of M. The sum of components (a) and (b) is the reliable variance of M, and we may define by reference to it the characteristic P, which is the characteristic, or weighted compound of characteristics, which the scale actually measures. In the terms of this simple trichotomy, the analysis of a classification or scale consists in the solution of two problems. One is the question of the extent to which it measures what it is supposed to measure, and the other is the question of the extent to which it measures things which it is not supposed to measure.

Clearly if measuring instrument M measures external or objective characteristic X with a certain degree of random error, the reliability and hence the validity of M will be less than perfect. Since measurement error is inherent in all empirical research, we regard it as the duty of the constructor of an instrument to reduce random error to the extent that the nature of his field of inquiry permits and, having reached some sort of approximation to this limit, then to concentrate his attention on estimating the extent of error which remains.

The more important, and in practice more difficult, task in the analysis of M is that of finding out how far M measures characteristics other than X. If P is the characteristic or compound of characteristics measured by M (i.e. it is equivalent to M after the elimination of all random error) then this question becomes, to what extent is the association between P and X less than perfect and to what characteristic or characteristics other than X is P related? Of course, if P is a perfect measure of X then it will correlate with some other characteristic Y to the extent that X correlates with Y. Difficulties arise, however, when the correlation between P and X is rendered less than perfect by a bias in P towards Y.

In the following two sections of this chapter existing classifications and scales of occupations are examined. We first ask a basic question concerning the extent to which an underlying occupational attribute P is identifiable with some characteristic X of which instrument M is purportedly a pure measure—i.e. we impugn the validity of interpreting occupation scales as unbiased measures of a truly sociological characteristic such as 'prestige' or 'social standing'. Then we discuss existing scales in the light of the accuracy with which instrument M allocates individuals to categories of, or points on, attribute P—i.e. the reliability of occupational grading schemes.

Validity

The question of the validity of a classification or scale is that of how well it orders items according to the characteristic or 'dimension' to which it is supposed to relate. By extension, one can think of this issue as being that of the validity of the *inferences* that the classification or scale will lead one to make.

For example, the five 'Social classes' recognized by the Office of Population Censuses and Surveys (OPCS), which are used in the analysis of many official statistics, are a classification of occupations (or, to be precise, of 'unit groups' of occupations) according to 'the general standing within the community of the occupations concerned'. Again, the OPCS 'Socio-economic groups' are also an occupationally based classification which aims to bring together 'people whose social, cultural and recreational standards and behaviour are similar' (Office of Population Censuses and Surveys, 1970, p. x). Such classifications, pertaining as they do to what sociologists might wish to term 'prestige' and 'life-style', are ones of obvious *prima facie* attractiveness and utility. However, one must ask: if one inferred, following these classifications, that individuals placed in one Social class or Socio-economic group have superior or inferior prestige or different life-styles to individuals placed in another, how valid would these inferences prove to be in the light of a direct empirical investigation of 'the standing in the community' or the 'social, cultural and recreational standards and behaviour' of the individuals concerned? In other words, how far is the 'manifest' attribute— membership of an occupational group—on which the classifications actually rest, a valid and unbiased indicator of the 'latent' attributes to which the classifications claim to refer? (For futher discussion of the manifest/latent relationship see Galtung, 1967, pp. 29, 122–7, 274–82.) In fact, acquaintance with studies of particular occupations, and with studies of local status structures and patterns of subcultural variation within modern Britain must give rise to doubts about the validity of these classifications. Certainly, no results from attempts to validate them have ever been reported. Thus one can place no more reliance on them than one would intuitively place on the common-sense knowledge and armchair decision-making ability of the officials responsible for their construction.

Moreover, it must not be supposed that empirical investigation in itself represents any automatic method of resolving problems of validity. This point may be illustrated by consideration of those classifications and scales developed by sociologists themselves specifically for the measurement of occupational prestige. Typically, in the construction of these instruments, an inquiry has been conducted into the popular assessment of the prestige of some sample of occupations by asking respondents to rate or rank occupation titles according to their 'prestige', 'social standing', 'social status', or other such-like criterion. The results of these inquiries have then been taken either as constituting a test of the validity of some pre-established scale, as with the British 'Hall-Jones' scale (Hall and Jones, 1950; Moser and Hall, 1954) or, as in the case of the National Opinion Research Centre (Reiss, 1961) and other American studies, as a basis for the more comprehensive 'scoring' of occupations through the use of various methods of 'interpolation' (Cf. Duncan, 1961, pp. 110–12).

The procedures in question here are open to several far from trivial objections even when taken on their own terms.* But, leaving these aside, it can also be argued, as we have done elsewhere (Goldthorpe and Hope, 1972), that the validity of classifications and scales thus based is open to far more radical doubt.

To summarize our argument, if 'prestige' is to be understood in any way approximating to its established sense within the sociological tradition, then it must refer to the position of an individual or group within a structure of relations of deference, acceptance and derogation, which represents a distinctive, 'symbolic' aspect of social stratification. Relative advantage and power in terms of prestige stem from the ability of an actor to exploit and benefit from *meanings* and *values*–rather than, say, economic resources, authority, or physical force. From this standpoint, therefore, occupational prestige must derive from certain symbolic significance, relevant to ideas of social superiority or inferiority, which the incumbency of an occupational role or membership of an occupational collectivity conveys. And so a measure of occupational prestige is to be regarded as valid to the extent that one may correctly infer from it the relative chances that a member of an occupational category has of experiencing deference, acceptance, or derogation in his relations with members of other categories.

Regrettably, the issue of validation posed in this form appears to have been recognized by only one previous investigator (Svalastoga, 1959, pp. 120–3) and, in the event, the test which he is able to apply to his scale cannot be regarded as convincing. Most usually, it has been argued (Duncan and Artis, 1951, p. 21; Reiss, 1961, pp. 190–2) that the validity of an occupational prestige scale inheres simply in the extent to which raters or rankers display concurrence[†] in their assessments of occupations. However, while a large measure of such agreement could certainly be regarded as a necessary condition for the validity of a prestige scale (since the symbols related to incumbency of an occupational role must, if they are to be effective, be generally recognized and similarly evaluated), this is

---

* For example, the Hall-Jones scale might be said to have been validated by the empirical enquiry into occupational prestige in the sense that the assessments made of occupations in terms of their 'social standing' produced evidence (i) that *some* publicly recognized hierarchy of occupations existed; and (ii) that the ordering of the scale categories in terms of 'high' and 'low' was broadly in accordance with this recognized hierarchy. However, three of the thirty titles graded appeared to require reclassification as a consequence of the results of the empirical enquiry, and, while this was done, the definitions of the scale categories do not appear to have been reviewed in the light of these changes, nor was any attempt made to estimate the degree of error incorporated in the scale over-all. For a criticism of 'interpolation' methods, see Duncan, 1961.

† A detailed discussion of the notions of 'concurrence' and 'consensus' as we would wish to use them in connection with occupational grading is provided in Appendix A, pp. 147ff.

not to say that it is a *sufficient* condition. The issue of what there is agreement about—of what occupational prestige ratings or rankings actually relate to—ought not to be burked. However, because this issue *has* in fact been neglected, one finds that often the meanings given to occupational prestige, and thus the interpretation of occupational prestige scales, are left uncertain if not confused;* and, furthermore, that writers are ready to make inferences from scale positions and movements for which no good grounds exist (see Goldthorpe and Hope, 1972, pp. 33—7 esp.). Indeed, it can be argued not only that conventional occupational prestige scales are *un*validated, but further, that evidence incidentally available indicates that they are quite probably *in*valid in that they measure prestige only to the degree that they measure attributes of occupations which are correlated with prestige.

First, one may note that when respondents who have performed a prestige rating or ranking task have been asked what in fact were the criteria they chiefly had in mind when assessing the occupations presented to them, the answers given have regularly indicated that only a small proportion had adopted a distinctively 'prestige' frame of reference; that is, one in which the respondent was sensitive to the specifically symbolic significance of occupational attributes as determining the probable experience of their incumbents in relations of deference, acceptance and derogation. (See Taft, 1953; Tiryakian, 1958; Reiss, 1961, pp. 31—7.) The majority of respondents seem, rather, to have emphasized the relevance of job rewards or job requirements *per se* and, as one investigator has acknowledged, 'do not appear to have made their evaluations in terms of a conscious awareness of the social prestige attached to the occupation' (Reiss, 1961, p. 37).

Secondly, it may be observed that in studies of this kind the degree of agreement among individuals on the grading of occupations appears to be little affected by the respondent's location within the social structure. That is to say, individuals from the same collectivity—socio-economic, residential, regional, etc.— show no appreciable tendency to agree more with each other than do individuals from different collectivities. Since, then, the mean correlation between pairs of graders is usually about 0·5 or 0·6, the mean gradings of a sample from one social collectivity frequently correlate well over 0·9 with the mean gradings of a sample from another collectivity—just as would the means of two quite random samples. These findings are difficult to understand if a 'prestige' dimension is indeed being tapped. For in this case one might expect that at least *some* part of any inter-individual dissensus that occured would be accountable for in terms of socially structured differences in meaning and values which would then also be revealed at the collective level. We have evidence (see, for example, Hyman, 1954; Kohn, 1969; Mann, 1970) that values and symbols do vary with socio-economic status in modern industrial societies, and these variations might well

---

*Perhaps the most frequent source of confusion lies in shifts made from a 'strong' usage of 'prestige'—i.e. in its established sociological sense—to some much weaker one, equating it with, say, 'socio-economic status'. The former usage typically occurs in the discussion of some substantive sociological issue; the latter, when the writer self-consciously considers how his 'prestige' scale might most realistically be interpreted.

be supposed to manifest themselves in differences between collectivities in the relative prestige ascribed to occupations.* Again, then, the suggestion must be that the grading tasks on which conventional occupational prestige scales rest do not in the main succeed in evoking the kind of response that their 'face value' interpretation would imply.[†]

Reliability

The reliability of data may be formally defined as the degree to which the variance they contain is 'true' variance and not the outcome of classificatory or measurement 'error'.

In the case of occupational classifications the first problem of reliability arises from the fact that there are many thousands of different occupations—the OPCS index (1970) recognizes well over 20,000—which a classification intended for general use must be able to accommodate. In the course of applying such a classification, specific occupations have to be allocated—that is 'coded'—to one or other of the categories that are provided. What, ideally, is desired is that every occupation should, following coding instructions, be invariably coded to the same category each time that it is encountered. To the extent that this requirement is met, the classification made will be reliable. In practical terms, then, the problem is one of producing instructions which ensure that those carrying out the coding operation regularly agree both with themselves and with other coders in the codes that they give to particular occupations. It is, moreover, important to note that 'other coders' must extend here not simply to others within a single project but to all those who may at any time use the coding procedure. In other words, for a high level of reliability to be obtained, a classification scheme must be associated with coding instructions of a sufficiently public, specific, and detailed character to make possible a high degree of both intra- and inter-subjective consistency, even where initially 'naïve' coders are employed.

In fact, this requirement has often been neglected. For example, as Macdonald has pointed out (1974), the instructions followed in coding occupations into the Hall-Jones scale on the first occasion of its use (Glass, 1954) have never been published. For long, in fact, the only information available to other intending users of the scale was the category descriptions, together with the allocation of the set of 30 titles for which 'prestige' ratings were empirically established. The category descriptions in themselves are obviously inadequate to define a coding frame; and the titles assigned constitute weak reference points since they are

---

* All the more so since some evidence does exist specifically of 'status dissent' on the part of some groups of manual works. For Great Britain, see, for example, Willmott (1963) and Goldthorpe *et al.*, (1969).

† A further question is, of course, that of whether such a response could be evoked by *any* kind of task; i.e. of whether in modern societies an occupationally based prestige order does in fact exist that is sufficiently integrated, stable, and pervasive to be readily perceived by the majority of individuals. In the British case, for example, it can certainly be claimed that any such order must today appear greatly attenuated in comparison, say, with that prevailing in rural society in the last century (Cf. Thompson, 1963, chs. i-v esp.).

few in number and would seem to be unrepresentative of the distribution of occupations in a modern industrial society. Sixteen years after the scale was constructed, Oppenheim (1966, pp. 275–84) published a list of some 650 occupation titles assigned to Hall-Jones categories, which, it appears, was used in some way in the initial application of the scale. Even this, however, is of only limited value so far as the reliability of coding is concerned. For, as Oppenheim admits, the list 'contains only a fraction of the job names that exist'–in fact, only about one in thirty on the basis of the OPCS index–and while it may include 'most of the occupations that are encountered frequently in survey work', the proportion of *all* occupations encountered which is *not* covered by the list must still be sizeable.

Thus, as Macdonald has argued, the sense in which it can be said that the Hall-Jones scale has been 'widely used' in social research in Britain (Bechhofer, 1969, p. 113) is somewhat problematic. Certainly it cannot be assumed, given the inadequate guidance under which coders must have worked, that highly comparable classifications of occupations have been produced wherever the name of the scale has been invoked. How far coders have achieved consistency from one study to another in assigning occupations to Hall-Jones categories is not known;* and neither, it may be added, have we been able to discover any published estimate of the degree of coder reliability *within* any particular application of the scale.

In the case of occupational classifications which aim to be no more than 'nominal', or in which an ordering is introduced by *fiat* or by reference to quite external criteria, problems of reliability do not extend beyond the coding operation.† However, where in the construction of an occupational scale its categories are given numerical values on the basis of some empirical procedure– for example, an occupational prestige inquiry or the analysis of census data– then the problem of reliability takes on a different aspect. On the one hand, correctness of coding will not guarantee the reliability of the scale values and, on the other hand, errors of coding will not necessarily be reflected in errors in scale values.

A study which is concerned with the standing of occupational roles must abstract from any differences in the personal standing of individuals who share

---

* We have, however, ourselves been able to make one small investigation on this point. Professor Bertram Hutchinson has kindly made available to us the Hall-Jones codes which he and his co-workers assigned to some 600 occupations encountered in a study of social mobility in Dublin (see Hutchinson, 1969). These occupations of course, overlap to some extent with the 650 or so in Oppenheim's list, but were coded without direct reference to that list. Thus it is that in the case of 355 occupations we can compare the independent Hall-Jones codings of two separate teams. The number of occupations on which there is a disagreement over category is 16 and these include such fairly common occupations as railway porter, shop assistant, hotel waiter, sanitary inspector, and bank manager. That differences in coding rules can lead to relatively large differences in occupational mobility tables has been demonstrated by Taubman (1973).

† That is, from the point of view of the classification itself. Other problems may arise as a consequence of the quality of the information from which respondents' occupations are determined.

a common role. If we leave these individual differences out of account, our first task is to assess the extent to which occupations, all of which have been assigned by the coding procedure to a single category and hence to a single point on the scale, are diverse in their 'true' projections on to the scale. If the scale score for the category is, let us say, the mean of the scores of all occupations in the category (or of some sample of them) then the standard deviation from this mean will offer some indication of the amount of 'error' which occurs in assigning the same category score to all occupations that the category comprises.

Furthermore, if it is the case that the scores for particular occupations, which provide the basis for category scores, are themselves derived from public assessments of occupational 'prestige', 'social standing', or the like, then two other considerations also become relevant for the question of reliability: the extent to which respondents are constant in their ratings or rankings of occupations— that is, agree with themselves from one time to another; and the extent to which, on average, they agree with one another. Were it to be found that respondents are highly inconstant in their assessments, or display considerable dissensus, then statistical means would have to be devised for reducing the effect of such error on the scale values produced from ratings or rankings.*

In fact, few occupation scales giving numerical values have thus far been developed[†]—and none has been constructed for Great Britain. The immediately preceding remarks are thus not so much criticisms of existing practice as a foretaste of the problems which we had to meet in our own undertaking.

* Though if the degree of dissensus proved to be very great the validity of the procedure would be in doubt.
† The best-known is that which Duncan (1961) constructed on the basis of U.S. Census data in order to make it possible to give estimated NORC 'prestige' scores to all occupations officially recognized.

2. THE APPROACH TO PROBLEMS OF VALIDITY

The choice of possibilities

The attempt to solve the problems of validity posed by existing occupational prestige scales could, it would seem, follow one or other of two courses.

One possibility would be to seek to develop new occupational prestige scales which have greater demonstrated validity in the sense that we have insisted upon; that is, which can be shown to sanction relatively accurate inferences concerning the experience of members of different occupational categories in relations of deference, acceptance, or derogation. Some attempts in this direction have in fact already been made and others are in progress. The essential difference between this approach and the conventional one is that the empirical basis of the scale is not the relative position of occupations in popular assessments of their 'prestige', etc., but the degree to which members of different occupational groups do actually engage with each other in some particular form of intimate association, such as, say, marriage or close friendship. In this case, then, the 'manifest' attribute being studied would appear to be a good deal closer to the 'latent' attribute which is of ultimate interest; and, moreover, various techniques of analysis are available which can help determine how far frequencies of marriage or friendship between members of different occupational groups can in fact be seen as the product of some single underlying dimension.* Indeed, in this

* The techniques to which we refer are those which are associated with the dimensional analysis of a contingency table, and they fall into two main classes: the generally non-metric methods associated with the title 'multidimensional scaling' (e.g. Laumann and Guttman, 1966), and the metric methods whose axes are the explanatory or canonical dimensions of canonical regression (Hope, 1972, pp. 123ff.). Leaving aside the question of the relative merits of the two approaches (which is briefly discussed on p. 166 of the paper of Hope cited) we may note that the attempt to locate occupations on a scale by analysis of a contingency table creates certain difficulties. The first problem to be faced is that the cells of the table may (for reasons which would not be without sociological interest) depart from symmetry to a degree which precludes the assignment of occupations to positions on a single scale. The second problem is that the mode of association (marriage, friendship, etc.) for which the table was compiled will almost certainly reflect a number of determining factors in addition to prestige. And the third is that the construction of a prestige scale by analysis of a particular mode (e.g. occupational mobility) may introduce a degree of contamination between independent and dependent variables into studies which employ the scale as an axis for the study of that mode.

We suggest that the spatial analysis of contingency tables is an excellent technique for the substantive study of social consequences of prestige, locality and networks, but that it is an imperfect device for the construction of an axis of the 'stratification space' (Hope, 1972, pp. 1ff.) within which social relations are anchored to the positions of the role-incumbents among whom they effect links. And the imperfections are such that it would be very difficult to detect and estimate their effects, as we have been able to estimate the errors in our occupation grading scale. The very fact that the techniques of dimensional analysis frequently discover a first dimension which is significantly larger than the second and subsequent dimensions is probably a consequence of the overdetermination of the main axis by several factors. Employment of these methods leads inevitably to problems of rotation and reification of axes (see Macdonald, 1972) analogous to those which have largely discredited factor analysis as a means for test construction in spite of its theoretical elegance way it may be possible to investigate the basic question raised earlier (p. 7 above, note), of whether, in a modern industrial society, an occupationally based prestige order is sufficiently clearly recognized to enable it to exert a highly systematic influence on everyday social relations.

However, this approach is not the one that we ourselves adopted. Rather than beginning with the concept of occupational prestige and seeking more valid ways of measuring it, we decided to begin with the general pattern of results produced by existing occupation grading studies and to seek for more valid ways of interpreting them. Two grounds for this decision may be stated. First, from the point of view of the inquiry into occupational mobility with which we were concerned, a scale of occupational prestige *stricto sensu* would not be of as great utility as one relating to some rather less specific occupational attribute. Secondly, the findings of existing studies—in particular, the apparent absence of any kind of socially structured dissensus on the grading of occupations—revealed a degree and kind of regularity unusual in social research. These data, we believed, could not be disregarded simply because in the past they had often been construed in an unwarranted manner.

Occupation 'prestige' reconsidered

The questions which we posed for ourselves were, then, these: What do occupational prestige scales, as conventionally constructed, actually measure? Within what frame or frames of reference do individuals operate when asked to rate or rank occupation titles according to their 'prestige', 'social standing', etc.? The answers that we suggested (Goldthorpe and Hope, 1972, pp. 30–2) may be summarized as follows.

When individuals are confronted with the kind of grading task on which conventional studies of occupational prestige are based, this does *not*, in the majority of cases, lead them to adopt a distinctively 'prestige' frame of reference; that is, a frame of mind in which they respond primarily in terms of symbolic indications of social superiority or inferiority. Rather, most respondents assess the occupations presented to them on the basis of what they know, or think they know, about a *variety* of more 'objective' occupational attributes—most often, perhaps, job rewards or requirements*—which they see as relevant to the ordering of occupations *simply in terms of some rather unspecific 'better-worse' dimension*. Different respondents operate with different attributes in mind and may perhaps be thought of, when using more than one attribute, as differing in the subjective 'weights' they attach to them in arriving at their assessments. Thus the scales which result from occupational 'prestige' grading exercises may best be taken as representing a synthetic and 'emergent' judgement from the population concerned; a judgement which is indicative of what might be called the

---

for the conceptual analysis of test variance. (For a development of this thesis, see Hope, 1972, p. 121ff.)

* As their own accounts would largely suggest. See the references cited in ch. 1, p. 6 above.

'general goodness', or as we would now prefer to phrase it, the 'general desirability' of occupations.

Given *this* understanding of 'prestige' scores we may note, first of all, that the argument for their validity advanced by Duncan and Artis and by Reiss (see above, p. 5) can now be applied with much greater force than when it is used to justify their acceptance at face value: that is, the argument that the usefulness of such scales lies in the degree of concurrence which is, as a matter of fact, found in assessments of occupations—notwithstanding any differences among respondents in their evaluative procedures. For in the interpretation suggested it is no longer being claimed that the scales obtained from respondents' assessments of occupational 'prestige' tap some underlying structure of social relations—that is, a prestige order—and thus justify inferences about attitudes and behaviour within the context of this structure. Rather, the potential interest of such scales *lies directly in their ability to display* the convergence of—or, one might say, the extent of the 'common factor' in—popular assessments of occupations, according to *whatever* attributes individuals happen to regard as relevant to the position of occupations in over-all 'better-worse' terms.*

In turn, then, it does now become arguable that the crucial issue, so far as validity is concerned, is not the degree of respondents' evaluative consensus but rather that of whether all those attributes of occupations to which respondents tend to refer are, as perceived, themselves sufficiently inter-correlated to make assessments of particular occupations broadly similar, however respondents may vary in the specific attributes they focus on or emphasize. In fact, though, as our own empirical work enables us to show (see Appendix A. p. 144) it is not necessary to rely exclusively on assumptions about the extent of correlation among perceived attributes of occupations. Over and above the effect of such correlation it is at least possible that agreement on 'prestige' gradings may also have a consensual element in that respondents may, in grading a set of occupations, implicitly ascribe similar relative weights to the various attributes which they take into account. In this way, therefore, a level of agreement may be achieved which is appreciably *higher* than the inter-correlation that exists among the occupational attributes themselves. However, it is important to add that, in our interpretation, the consensus in question does *not* have to be taken as implying—as it would have to be in a 'prestige' interpretation—some shared pattern of response to symbols of general social superiority and inferiority. It may be regarded simply as consensus on the relative importance of different features of occupations in contributing to their standing in terms of 'general desirability'.

---

* This suggests that the particular criterion in terms of which individuals are asked to grade occupations has no very specific meaning for them, or, perhaps, is not taken very seriously by them, but serves simply to trigger off a grading operation of the kind that is being suggested. Such a view is supported by the fact that some appreciable degree of variation in the actual wording of the criterion can take place without, apparently, making any significant difference to the results achieved: e.g. 'prestige' 'social prestige', 'social standing', 'social status', and 'desirability' would all seem to be highly interchangeable. Cf. Hodge *et al.* (1966).

As well as fitting in with respondents' own accounts of how they actually perform 'prestige' rating or ranking exercises, the interpretation of their results that we propose has one further advantage which may be noted: that of making less puzzling than in a face-value interpretation the absence of disagreement which is of a socially structured kind. The extent to which agreement among individuals is less than complete (mean correlations for pairs of graders are about 0·5 or 0·6) may be plausibly seen as reflecting, first, differences in knowledge about particular occupations (and perhaps other sources of 'error'), and secondly, the degree of dissensus among individuals in their choice and weighting of the attributes which they treat as relevant to occupational desirability. There is, then, little reason to expect that disagreement arising in *these* ways *should* be socially structured in any striking degree.* Knowledge about the more general characteristics of other than rather esoteric occupations is relatively 'open'; and it is in general unlikely that ideas about what things are 'good' in a job would show any very marked social patterning.† It is not unreasonable to assume a minimal value consensus to the effect that, by and large, high pay will be preferred to low, more security to less, pleasant work conditions to unpleasant ones, autonomy to close control, and so on. Consequently, individual differences should to a large extent 'cancel out' both within and between collectivities, and thus produce the very high measure of agreement on the 'average' assessment of occupations that is regularly observed.

Understood in this way, it may be added, such agreement not only ceases to be surprising but, at the same time, loses the importance with which functionalist theoreticians have sought to invest it (see, for example, Barber, 1957, p. 6); that is, as demonstrating that the factual order of stratification in modern societies is generally consistent with the prevailing normative order. Rather, the data in question must be regarded as having little normative—at least in the sense of 'legitimatory'—significance at all. What can be taken as indicated is simply the theoretically neutral—though practically highly convenient—fact that from one socio-economic stratum, age group, residential class, region, etc. to another, assessments of the 'general desirability' of occupations work out, on average, to be very much the same.‡

Thus it is possible to advance an explanation of occupational 'prestige' scales which is more consonant than a face-value interpretation with our existing

---

*Except, perhaps, in the special and very limited cases where respondents are assessing occupations within their own status or situs areas. Cf. Blau (1957) and Gerstl and Cohen (1964).
† Note that the subject of discussion here is *not* the range of considerations—many of them perhaps relatively specific to particular groups or strata—which would arise in an individual's own job choice.
‡ The theoretically interesting situation would be that where this was *not* the case. This would imply the existence of structured dissensus—among strata or age groups or other collectivities—on what are generally taken to be desirable and undesirable features of occupations. In such a situation a scale purporting to measure the general desirability of occupations could only represent some sort of compromise among the conceptions of the various collectivities.

knowledge of the construction procedures and properties of such scales. None the less, further investigation specifically designed to explore, and quantify the components of, the model underlying this new interpretation seemed to us to be desirable. Primarily for this purpose, we devised and carried out the occupation grading study—referred to for convenience as the Oxford inquiry—which is described in detail in Appendix A. Here it will be sufficient to note the major features of this study and to report those of its findings which are directly relevant to the concerns of this chapter.

The Oxford inquiry

The study was based on two randomly selected samples of the electorate of the city of Oxford (excluding 'S' voters* and voters who were shown as having their eighteenth birthday during the life of the electoral register). An occupational prestige grading task of a conventional type was administered to members of one of the samples. Forty occupations were to be ranked in order of what respondents believed to be their *Social standing*—the same criterion as that used in the Hall-Jones inquiry. To the other sample, however, was allocated a task of a more novel and complex kind. Forty occupations—the same list as for the first sample—were to be ranked according to four different criteria: namely, the *Standard of living, Power and influence over other people* and *Level of qualifications* that their members possess, and their *Value to society*. Furthermore, in this case, the grading task was to be repeated in identical form between two and three months after it had first been carried out.

With this design, it was open to us to test two hypotheses of major interest for our purposes.

(1) That respondents performing the second, 'four-dimensional' task, while differing to some extent among themselves in their assessments of occupations on the four 'dimensions' or attributes, would none the less as a whole—i.e. on average—discriminate in their application of the dimensions, even though correlations among the dimensions might be substantial.

(2) That respondents performing the first, 'one-dimensional' task, while also differing to some extent among themselves, would produce average scores for occupations in terms of 'social standing' which could be very closely approximated by a linear combination of the positions of the occupations on the four attributes graded by the second sample.

In so far, then, as these hypotheses might be upheld, the interpretation of conventional occupational prestige scales which we have advanced would receive further corroboration.

The relevant findings derived from the study can be stated as follows:

(i) In the four-dimensional sample ($n = 160$) the extent of agreement among individuals' gradings on each of the four dimensions was, as expected, at only

---

* An 'S' against the name of a registered voter indicates that he is serving in the Armed Forces.

a moderate level. The average correlations of the scores produced by any two respondents were as follows: on Standard of living (S), 0·58; on Power and influence (I), 0·55; on Level of qualifications (Q), 0·64; and on Value to society (V), 0·46.

(ii) Again as anticipated, the average scores received by occupations on the different dimensions were intercorrelated—although with some notable variation in strength. The full correlation matrix is given in Table A4. It may be observed that while three correlations (r_{SQ}, r_{IQ} and r_{IV}) are over 0·85, two others (r_{SI} and r_{QV}) are about 0·75 and the remaining correlation (r_{SV}) falls below 0·50.*

(iii) The departures from perfect association cannot be attributed to simple error. Analysis of the variance of the gradings reveals, as one would expect, that the major factor is simply the differences among the grades assigned to occupations. This component, accounting for 42 per cent of the total, represents those aspects of the distinctions among occupations which are common among graders and general among the attributes. These distinctions are almost exactly reproduced on the second occasion of grading. However, a further 13 per cent of the total variance is attributable to the distinctions which the average member of the sample makes among the four attributes, and the pattern of these distinctions is also repeated with almost perfect accuracy on the second occasion of grading. Furthermore, another 9 per cent of the variance is attributable to distinctions which represent individual graders' personal discriminations among the attributes in so far as these differ from the sample average. We conclude, therefore, not only that graders can distinguish among attributes of occupations, but also that the extent to which they agree with one another in making particular distinctions is somewhat greater than their tendency to disagree. The shared discriminations are highly stable, at least over an interval of a few weeks.

(iv) All the results reported above hold good for sub-sets of the four-dimensional sample, whether the sub-sets are constituted in terms of respondent's occupation, age, or sex. Furthermore, no marked difference between sub-sets is found, on any dimension, in the gradings of occupations. The breakdown of the sample which might have been thought most likely to produce significant differences among collectivities is that in terms of occupational level of respondent, and the negative results of this analysis are reported in Tables A5 to A8 of Appendix A.†

(v) Respondents in the sample ($n = 65$) which ranked the 40 occupation titles in terms of their 'social standing' produced gradings which are entirely typical

* Our results in this respect are thus consistent with the arguments and findings of Rossi and Inkeles (1957), who were probably the first to question the view of psychologists such as Asch *et al.* (1938) and Osgood and Stagner (1941) that the existence of some fixed 'frame of reference' or 'general standard' leads to individuals assigning a similar grading to any given occupation regardless of the dimension on which it is being assessed.

† In fact the only respect in which we ourselves expected to find significant differences among occupational collectivities was in the grading of occupations on the 'value to society' attribute where an essentially evaluative, as opposed to a cognitive, judgement would seem to be unavoidable (cf. Goldthorpe and Hope, 1972, pp. 39–40). This expectation was not fulfilled but the outcome was not unwelcome since it made our analytic task easier than it might otherwise have been.

of this conventional task. While agreement at the individual level is modest—the average correlation between the gradings of pairs of respondents is 0·46—a high level of agreement exists among the means of the occupational collectivities which are distinguished.

(vi) The vector of mean gradings of the forty occupations by this latter sample is, to the extent of 97 per cent of its variance, a linear combination of the vectors of the mean gradings on the four attributes by the other sample. Indeed, the correlation between the mean gradings of the 'one-dimensional' sample and the simple means of the 'four-dimensional' sample over all respondents and attributes is 0·98. As Figure 1 shows, 'social standing' is virtually the centroid of the four attributes that were distinguished.

Figure 1 may in fact serve as a convenient summary of the main findings of the Oxford inquiry that are relevant to our present purposes. While the results there displayed cannot of course conclusively confirm the interpretation that we would give to occupational prestige scales—that is, that they reflect a composite popular judgement of the 'general desirability' of occupations—they are at all events highly consistent with it.* To adopt such an interpretation may well appear to offer fewer sociological possibilities than, say, taking prestige scales at face value, or as in some way reflecting a dominant social ideology (cf. Ridge, 1974). But—and this must commend it to the empirical researcher—it is the interpretation which would seem to offer the best guarantee against the drawing of unwarranted and possible misleading inferences when such a scale is being applied.

* See also in this connection the results reported by Rossi and Inkeles (1957).

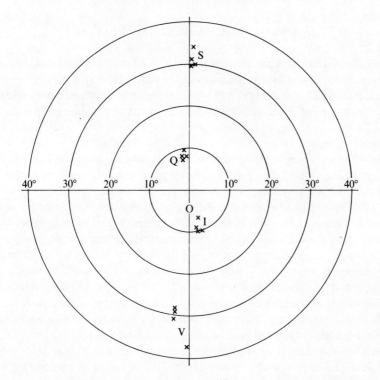

Fig. 1. Plot of the projections of four attributes of occupations on to a spherical surface. Each quadruplet of points represents an attribute as assessed by four occupational categories of respondent. The distal points for S and V are those for the category of students. O is the projection of gradings of the 'social standing' of occupations by a further sample of respondents.

3. THE APPROACH TO PROBLEMS OF RELIABILITY

As we indicated in chapter 1, the first problem of reliability in the classification of occupations is that of *coder disagreement and inconsistency* in identifying a particular occupation as belonging to a basic element of the classificatory scheme that is being applied. We shall call such basic elements 'occupation grading units'. Where these units are aggregated so as to form larger occupational categories, the process of aggregation may, of course, be carried out entirely automatically. If one introduces a scaling method whereby all occupation grading units, and hence all occupations, falling into a particular category are given the same scale value, one must then take cognizance of a second type of unreliability: namely, the extent of diversity or *heterogeneity* within a category in the 'true' projections of its constituent occupations on to the characteristic measured approximately by the scale. This heterogeneity has two components: the diversity of occupations assigned to an occupation grading unit, and the diversity of occupation grading units assigned to a category. Thirdly, in constructing any occupational scale which is based on popular assessments—whether of 'prestige', of 'social standing', or of any other characteristic—it is necessary to take account of the extent to which, in the empirical grading inquiry, there is *disagreement among respondents* in their judgement of the positions of occupations. And lastly, as the technical argument of Appendix A shows, in order to estimate the extent of such disagreement, it is necessary to be able to estimate also the degree to which departures from complete concurrence are inflated by *respondent inconsistency*.

The following sections outline the general principles that guided us in dealing with these various sources of error and unreliability.

Disagreement and inconsistency in coding

As we have previously argued, the essential requirement for a high level of reliability in the coding of occupations is that the assignment of particular occupations to the basic elements of a classification—the occupation grading units—should be governed by coding instructions that are of a public, specific, and detailed kind. In principle, one might perhaps conceive of an exhaustive directory of occupation descriptions and titles, for every entry in which the appropriate code would be indicated. Coding would then become simply a matter of looking up occupations that were encountered and of automatically recording their category as shown, so that the possibility of coders disagreeing with one another, or being inconsistent with themselves, would be eliminated. In practice, of course, no directory could ever attain completeness, since there is a practically infinite variety of ways in which occupations may be defined, and the exercise of some degree of judgement in the coding operation is inevitable.

None the less, in the interests of minimizing error, it should still, we believe, be regarded as a major *desideratum* of a coding system that it should combine assignment rules with the provision of an occupational directory which is as comprehensive as possible. The allocation of occupations to grading units may then be carried out primarily by a look-up method, which is clearly less error-prone than the alternative of providing verbal descriptions of categories supplemented by lists of exemplary occupations. When we embarked on our work there existed only one such coding system specifically devised for the United Kingdom; and that was the system of the Office of Population Censuses and Surveys, which incorporates the index of some 20,000 occupation titles to which we have already referred. We decided therefore to adopt some version of this system as the basis of our scale;* that is, to define our occupation grading units—the constituents of our scale categories—in such a way that occupations could be coded into them by means of OPCS procedures. The way in which this was done is described in detail in the following chapter.

By adopting the OPCS procedures we gained the additional advantage of being able to construct our scale in such a manner that its categories may be mapped into all three of the higher-level occupationally based classifications that the OPCS has established: the Social classes, the Socio-economic groups, and the Socio-economic classes. The following chapter shows how this possibility has been exploited.

Heterogeneity within a category

Since the number of occupation titles runs into tens of thousands, it is evident that the values of an occupational scale must in fact relate not to particular occupations but rather to groupings of occupations—either the grading units into which occupations are initially coded or, more practically, aggregations of these. Hence a further source of unreliability is introduced into the scale in that the occupations brought together in a scale category, and thus given the same scale value, will tend inevitably to be in some degree heterogeneous in their 'true' position on the scale. Moreover, obvious difficulties may arise in the application of a scale if the degree of diversity of its categories varies markedly along its length. In attacking these problems—which have received little previous attention— we sought to achieve two main objectives.

The first was the obvious one of defining our occupation grading units, and forming our scale categories from these units, so that the internal heterogeneity of both should be minimized. Since we intended our scale to be one based on popular assessments of (what we would interpret as) the 'general desirability' of occupations, it was necessary for us to try to anticipate such assessments as accurately as possible so as to group together occupations or grading units which would be accorded similar standing. One way of supplementing our own judgement

---

* Subsequently, a new British system, Classification of Occupations and Directory of Occupational Titles or 'Codot' (Department of Employment, 1972) appeared, but too late for us to consider using it. Another system which was available to us was that of the *International Standard Classification of Occupations* (ILO, 1968). This was, however, less suitable than the OPCS system for use in Britain, but it may be noted that the latter is broadly comparable with the two-digit level of the international classification.

A/ 301.55
305.5

in this respect was to recruit the services of experts; that is, persons with special-ized knowledge of the distribtuion of those occupational attributes—income, qualifications, work conditions, work relations, etc.—to which respondents in occupational grading inquiries would seem to give greatest weight.

At the same time, though, we recognized that all *a priori* attempts at reducing within-category diversity would in some degree be seen to have failed in the light of the eventual empirical results. So our second objective was to measure in some way the degree of diversity that we were unable to prevent, and in particular to ascertain how far this diversity varied from one category to another. The grading inquiry that we conducted was therefore designed to make possible the estimates of heterogeneity within scale categories which are reported in chapter 5. These estimates cannot give an entirely reliable idea of the absolute level of within-category diversity since they relate only to gradings of occupation *titles* chosen to be representative of a category, and not to gradings of the occupations of a random sample of *men* from each category. None the less, they do provide some general indication of the degree of success we achieved in seeking to maximize homogeneity within, and heterogeneity between, our categories, and they may be taken as a good—and in the event reassuring—guide to the extent to which category diversity is uniform along the length of our scale.

Respondent disagreement

The extent to which two respondents disagree in the assessment of an occu-pation in terms of its 'prestige' or 'social standing' is known to be considerable. In other words, the standard error of estimate of an occupation's position is high. Indeed, our own findings, reported in chapter 5, indicate that the variance of respondents grading the same occupation is much greater than the variance of the scale values of our categories.*

However, several pilot studies which we carried out prior to our grading inquiry revealed that, despite this extent of respondent disagreement, a moder-ately high degree of reliability could in fact be attained by averaging the gradings of an occupation over a relatively small number of respondents. By increasing the number of graders per occupation one could, of course, always produce yet higher levels of reliability, but this may be unnecessarily costly. As already noted, the values of an occupational scale must in practice relate to categories rather than to particular occupations. Thus, where the scale values are to be determined by popular assessments, the estimate whose reliability it is important to maximize will in fact be one based, not on the gradings of a single occupation, but on those of a number of occupation titles, selected so as to represent a category. The most obvious estimate to take for the scale value of a category is its average grading, computed over all its representative occupations and over all respondents supply-ing gradings for those occupations. The unreliability of each scale value will then

---

* That is, the component of the variance of an individual grading which is due to respondent disagreement is higher than the component of the same variance which is due to the fact that the occupation belongs to a particular category.

include one component representing heterogeneity, or variance among the representative occupations, and another component representing disagreement, or variance among the individuals grading any particular representative occupation.

The optimum strategy in the construction of an occupational scale of the kind in question is, therefore, one which chooses that number of occupations to represent a category, and that number of respondents to grade each occupation, which will, acting jointly, minimize the unreliability of the overall category mean which is to be the scale value of *all* occupations comprised by the category. Results from pilot studies supported our general impression that it is desirable to obtain gradings of a fair number of occupations within each scale category, and that this aim should not be sacrificed to that of effecting marginal improvements in the reliability of the gradings of particular representative occupations by having each assessed by a large number of respondents. For these gradings will themselves be averaged when the scale value of a category is calculated.

Respondent inconsistency

The remaining source of error in the grading of occupations lies in the tendency of a respondent's gradings to change from one performance of the grading task to another. This again is a problem which has hitherto been largely neglected.

Since it is clearly not possible to eliminate error from this source, the main requirement must be to obtain an estimate of the extent of the inconsistency that occurs. The most obvious way in which this may be done is by requiring some proportion at least of the respondents in an occupational grading study to repeat the grading task on a second occasion, preferably with a different interviewer. In designing our own grading inquiry, we made provision, as will be seen, for repeat interviews of this kind.

Where the values of scale categories are to be determined from the gradings of a number of representative occupations, the possibility arises of *differential* inconsistencies in the gradings of the occupations within a category. However, while such effects may occur, they are likely to have little importance when differential inconsistency among categories is considered. We did not therefore think it necessary to aim to do more than furnish a single over-all estimate of the component of the variance of a grading which is attributable to respondent inconsistency.

4. THE CONSTRUCTION OF THE SCALE

Our object, expressed in the terms of the preceding two chapers, was to construct a scale, which we would interpret as a measure of the 'general desirability' of occupations, on which occupations of all economically active men could be projected with some small, uniform, and estimable degree of error. Our first problem was, therefore, to find some way of handling the many thousands of occupations identified by the OPCS, whose coding procedures we had decided to employ. The first step towards the solution of this problem was the definition of the basic 'atoms' of our classificatory system, that is, the occupation grading units.

Occupation grading units

The OPCS *Classification of Occupations, 1970* distinguishes 223 'unit groups' of occupations, and it provides a comprehensive index to aid in the assignment of occupations to these groups. The aim in constituting unit groups is described as that of bringing together occupations that are similar primarily in the nature of the work-tasks they involve—although with a variety of other factors, including skill, working conditions, and associated 'social and economic status', being perhap also taken into account (OPCS, 1970, p. vi). Despite this aim, however, it seemed to us that many unit groups were likely to prove quite heterogeneous in terms of the perceived 'general desirability' of their constituent occupations, and that some subdivision of them would be necessary to reduce this heterogeneity.

One such subdivision could be achieved by crossing the unit group classification by another OPCS 'economic activity' classification, namely, that in terms of employment status.* In its most detailed version (OPCS, 1970, p. vi—ix) this classification takes the following form:

A. Self-employed
   (1) Without employees
   (2) With employees
       (a) Large establishments (25 or more employees)
       (b) Small establishments (less than 25 employees)

B. Employees
   (1) Managers
       (a) Large establishments (25 or more employees)
       (b) Small establishments (less than 25 employees)
   (2) Foremen and supervisors
       (a) Manual
       (b) Non-manual

* This is one of four OPCS 'economic activity' classifications, the other three being 'unit group', 'industry', and 'economic position' (this last relates to states such as 'in employment' 'unemployed', 'sick', 'retired', etc.).

22

(3) Apprentices, articled pupils, formal trainees
(4) Family workers
(5) Employees n.e.c. (not elsewhere classified)

We recognized that to introduce employment status into the construction of our scale at this basic level would be to abrogate the common supposition that an occupation is a work-role and set of work-tasks which may be identified independently of the economic relations in which its incumbents are involved. However, it would seem that in a modern industrial society this abstraction is increasingly difficult to sustain—as is most evident, perhaps, in the description and analysis of managerial and supervisory occupations (cf. OPCS, 1970, p. vii). We also noted that most current occupational 'prestige' scales do in fact take employment status into account, if only in an *ad hoc* fashion, by qualifying certain occupation titles with terms such as 'self-employed', 'own business', 'freelance', 'foreman', etc. It appeared to us, therefore, that little would be lost, and that much might be gained, by systematically introducing employment status into our classification procedures.

In doing so, we abridged the OPCS classification in two minor respects: we ignored the distinction between manual and non-manual foremen and the distinctions among apprentices etc., family workers, and employees (n.e.c.). The sevenfold employment status classification which results, and the code numbers which we assigned to each status, are shown in Table 4.1.

TABLE 4.1

The employment status classification and code numbers used in the construction of the scale

Classification	Code number
Self-employed with 25 or more employees	1
Self-employed with less than 25 employees	2
Self-employed without employees	3
Manager in an establishment with 25 or more employees	4
Manager in an establishment with less than 25 employees	5
Foreman/Supervisor	6
Employee*	7

* This includes: Apprentices and Trainees
                  Family employees
                  Other employees

By crossing unit group and employment status in this way it seemed to us that we might arrive at a distribution of occupations among cells which would display an acceptable degree of within-cell homogeneity. These cells are our occupation grading units.* It should be noted that, following OPCS coding procedures, certain combinations of unit group and employment status are impermissible: for instance, certain occupation codes must be linked with a supervisory or

* The very minor modifications which we made to the OPCS unit group classification are noted below, pp. 72f.

managerial employment status code while others cannot be so linked. Thus, the number of cells actually available is a good deal smaller than the mathematically possible maximum. A listing of all permissible combinations of occupation and employment status codes, and thus of all occupation grading units, is provided in Table 6.5.

The formation of the scale categories

The definition of our occupation grading units in the manner described not only enabled us to relate OPCS coding procedures directly to the basic elements of our classificatory scheme; it also greatly facilitated the next task we faced, namely, the formation of categories of occupations from which representative occupation titles could be selected for empirical grading by members of a sample of the national population.

The OPCS superordinate groupings of occupations, such as the Social classes and Socio-economic groups, are, as we noted earlier, of rather doubtful validity. They represent, however, aggregations of intermediate groupings of occupations, each grouping consisting of a set of unit groups associated with a particular employment status or subset of employment statuses. No name is given by the OPCS to this level of classification, but its elements are indicated clearly enough by the layout of the table which constitutes Appendix B.2 of the *Classification of Occupations, 1970*. The first few lines of this table are reproduced on the facing page in order to illustrate its structure.

Examination of the groupings marked out by the horizontal rules in the table suggested that they would form a useful first approximation to the scale categories that we required. We therefore assigned numbers to them, for reference purposes, starting with 01 for the first group at the head of the table and ending with 45 for the last.*

By means of these groupings our occupation grading units could be organized in a manageable way; but the groupings were still too few and too internally heterogeneous to serve as the categories on which our scale would rest. Some subdivision of them was clearly required. Since no systematic information was available from OPCS or other sources which might have assisted in this operation, we decided to rely on the judgements of experts in the fields of labour economics, industrial sociology, and industrial relations. Four experts were consulted, and each was invited to disaggregate each of the 45 groupings into categories which would, in his estimation, be as homogeneous as possible in terms of *the net extrinsic and intrinsic, material and non-material rewards and deprivations typically associated with the occupations which they comprised.*[†] In breaking

---

* Following the ruled lines strictly, one would in fact arrive at 39 categories. However, at various places in the table (i.e. with S.E.G.s 1.2, 5.1, and 7) divisions of an entirely analogous kind are indicated by a double spacing instead of a line, and the additional 4 categories thus formed were included in our count. We also introduced a threefold 'employment status' division into the Armed Forces category (S.E.G. 16) and excluded the 'Inadequately described occupations' category (S.E.G. 17).

[†] We are indebted to Dr. N. Ellis, Dr. W. E. J. McCarthy, Dr. R. Martin, and Dr. D. Robinson for undertaking this task.

Details of Socio-economic groups and Social Classes in terms of Occupation unit and Employment Status groups

S.E.G. 1.1 Employers in industry, commerce, etc.–large establishments

(a) Social Class II Intermediate occupations
Employment status–Self employed with employees

154	Publicans, innkeepers
156	Proprietors, managers, boarding houses and hotels
206	Authors, journalists and related workers
207	Stage managers, actors, entertainers, musicians
208	Painters, sculptors and related creative artists

115	Deck, engineering officers and pilots, ship
117	Aircraft pilots, navigators and flight engineers
123	Inspectors, supervisors, transport
143	Proprietors and managers, sales
147	Garage proprietors
149	Finance, insurance brokers, financial agents

(b) Social Class III (N) Skilled occuapations–Non-manual
Employment status–Self employed with employees

150	Salesmen, services; valuers, auctioneers
159	Restaurateurs
171	Proprietors and managers, service, sport and recreation n.e.c.
218	Draughtsmen

139	Clerks, cashiers
140	Office machine operators
141	Typists, shorthand writers, secretaries
148	Commercial travellers, manufacturers' agents

(c) Social Class III (M) Skilled occupations–Manual
Employment status–Self employed with employees

061	Shoemakers and shoe repairers
062	Cutters, lasters, sewers, footwear, and related workers
063	Leather products makers n.e.c.
067	Warpers, sizers, drawers-in
068	Weavers
069	Knitters

007	Coal mine-workers underground
009	Workers below ground n.e.c.
013	Ceramic formers
014	Glass formers, finishers and decorators
015	Furnacemen, kilnmen, glass and ceramic
016	Ceramics' decorators and finishers

. . .

down the groupings into categories, the experts, each of whom worked independently of the others, were to be guided by the following considerations:

(1) The various rubrics of Appendix B.2, other than those indicating the unit groups within a category and the associated employment status or statuses, were to be disregarded. All such information (for example, Socio-economic group and Social class headings) was deleted from the materials supplied to the experts to assist them in performing their task.

(2) The disaggregation of the 45 groups was to be taken to a point where, in the expert's view, the homogeneity of the resulting categories was as great as could be achieved within the limits set by the degree of heterogeneity within the basic elements, i.e. the occupation grading units.

(3) No category formed within one of the 45 groupings was to be amalgamated with a category formed within another grouping, however alike two such categories might appear to be. (By this rule we ensured that the categories of our scale may be aggregated into all the superordinate OPCS classificatory systems. Nothing is lost by having categories with identical projections on the scale.)

We ourselves then collated the disaggregations of the experts in the light of two principles:

(1) where experts differed only in the fineness of their breakdown, we adopted the finest categories.

(2) where experts disagreed on the allocation of grading units to categories, we took the majority view, giving ourselves a casting vote in the event of a tie. At this stage, we also took the opportunity of introducing a number of further subdivisions into our categories, this time in terms of 'situs' within four broadly defined economic sectors: Fishing, Mining and Quarrying; Manufacturing; Construction; and Transport, Communications and Services. Although situs may be only marginally relevant to the task of ordering occupations according to their 'general desirability', it seemed worth while to render the categorization on which our scale is based appropriate to inquiries in which situs distinctions may be of some importance—for instance, epidemiological studies. Disaggregation in terms of situs appeared to be called for mainly within groupings comprising skilled and semi-skilled manual occupations with 'supervisory' or 'employee' employment status. The extent of the situs distinctions made can be gauged from the 'Descriptive Titles' given in Table 6.4.*

The procedures which have been described in this section yielded 125 categories as the basis of our scale; that is, as the categories from which a sample of occupation titles would be selected for empirical grading—and to which in turn numerical values, derived from these gradings, would be assigned. Each category was given a four-digit reference number. The first two digits are the numbers (01 to 45) which refer to the OPCS occupational grouping (from Appendix B.2 of the *Classification of Occupations, 1970*) in which a category

---

* A good deal of further situs discrimination is, of course, already built into the OPCS groupings—and hence into our scale. For example, agricultural, professional, and managerial occupations are all separately categorized. For a general discussion of the notion of situs, see Morris and Murphy (1959).

lies. Digits three and four refer to the subdivision of such a grouping which a category represents, starting with 01 for the first category formed within each grouping. Thus, category 3111 is the eleventh category within grouping 31. However, the distinction between the first two and the last two digits of a category reference number may for most practical purposes be ignored, and the number itself treated simply as a uniquely referring expression having no important arithmetic or ordinal implications. Table 6.1 is a look-up table for assigning an occupation grading unit to its appropriate scale category. The reference number of an occupation grading unit itself consists of seven digits:

digits 1—4 are the appropriate category number;

digits 5—7 are the defining occupation unit group number.

It should be evident, then, that we took some pains to arrive at a coherent, defensible, and automatic means of combining occupation grading units to form the categories of our scale. Nevertheless, it must be emphasized that the merit of this categorization does *not* rest on the procedures by which it was arrived at. For purposes of assessing the reliability of our scale, the categories may in fact be taken as a 'given'—an arbitrary set of rules for taking an economically active man and ascribing to him a number, or scale value, in virtue of his occupation and associated employment status. The reliability of these numbers, representing the projections of individuals on our scale, is indicated by the extent to which members of the public endorse our *a priori* efforts to ensure the homogeneity of our categories when they assess the 'social standing' of representative occupations drawn from the categories.

The selection of representative occupation titles

The ideal method of selecting occupation titles for empirical grading might have involved weighting the chance of a title being taken as representative of its category by the number of men employed in that occupation. Since, however, the extremely detailed statistical information that would have been necessary to proceed in this way was unavailable, an alternative approach had to be adopted.

A preliminary step was to produce a 'reversed' version of the OPCS index of occupation titles; that is, one in which titles were listed not in simple alphabetical order but rather alphabetically within their respective unit groups.* Using this compilation, one can readily inspect all the occupation titles that a particular unit group comprises. The range of occupations covered by any category is indicated (a) by the occupation titles listed under unit group headings in the reversed index, and (b) by the employment status or statuses which qualify all occupations in the category. On the basis of this information, we selected representative titles for each of our 125 categories according to the following rules:

* This was done by transferring all the entries in the index (i.e. occupation titles plus their unit group code number) onto punched cards and then sorting them into unit group order. We are indebted to the punching and operating staff of the Atlas Computer Laboratory at Chilton, Berkshire, for undertaking this work.

TABLE 4.2

The 860 representative occupation titles
employed in the main grading inquiry

Title	Reference number

Category 0101, employment status 1

Captain and owner of pleasure boats (with more than 25 employees)*	0101/115/0
Owner-pilot, air-freight firm (with more than 25 employees)	0101/117/1
Proprietor of large public house (with more than 25 employees)	0101/154/2
Proprietor of large hotel (with more than 25 employees)	0101/156/3
Proprietor of large private hotel (with more than 25 employees)	0101/156/4

Category 0102, employment status 1

Publicity organizer (own agency, with more than 25 employees)	0102/206/0
Public relations consultant (own firm, with more than 25 employees)	0102/206/1
Film producer (with more than 25 employees)	0102/207/2
Commercial artist (own firm with more than 25 employees)	0102/208/3
Shop designer (own firm with more than 25 employees)	0102/208/4

Category 0103, employment status 1

Stockbroker (partner in firm with more than 25 employees)	0103/149/0
Insurance broker (partner in firm with more than 25 employees)	0103/149/1
Mortgage agent (partner in firm with more than 25 employees)	0103/149/2
Merchant banker (partner in firm with more than 25 employees)	0103/149/3
Investment dealer (partner in firm with more than 25 employees)	0103/149/4

Category 0104, employment status 1

Bus and coach operator (with more than 25 employees)	0104/123/0
Diamond broker (with more than 25 employees)	0104/143/1
Export agent (own business with more than 25 employees)	0104/143/2
Owner of furniture store (with more than 25 employees)	0104/143/3
Owner of supermarket (with more than 25 employees)	0104/143/4
Wholesale greengrocer (with more than 25 employees)	0104/143/5
Coal merchant (with more than 25 employees)	0104/143/6
Dairy owner (with more than 25 employees)	0104/143/7
Builders' merchant (with more than 25 employees)	0104/143/8
Garage proprietor (with more than 25 employees)	0104/147/9

Category 0201, employment status 1

Debt collector (own agency, with more than 25 employees)	0201/139/0
Estate agent (own firm, with more than 25 employees)	0201/150/1
Travel agent (own firm, with more than 25 employees)	0201/150/2
Insurance agent (own firm, with more than 25 employees)	0201/150/3
Auctioneer and valuer (own firm, with more than 25 employees)	0201/150/4
Owner of advertising agency (with more than 25 employees)	0201/150/5
Catering contractor (own firm, with more than 25 employees)	0201/159/6
Restaurant owner (with more than 25 employees)	0201/159/7
Betting-shop owner (with more than 25 employees)	0201/171/8
Cinema proprietor (with more than 25 employees)	0201/171/9

Category 0301, employment status 1

Radio and TV engineer (own shops with more than 25 employees)	0301/024/0
Automobile engineer (own garages with more than 25 employees)	0301/041/1
Coach operator (own firm with more than 25 employees)	0301/120/2
Haulage contractor (own firm with more than 25 employees)	0301/122/3
Ladies hairdresser (man, own salon, with more than 25 employees)	0301/167/4

Category 0302, employment status 1

Steelwork erector (own firm with more than 25 employees)	0302/034/0
Plumbing and heating engineer (own firm with more than 25 employees)	0302/045/1

* The form of words used by OPCS is 'with 25 or more employees' but we did not wish to
  confuse our informants with pedantry.

Title	Reference number
Carpenter and joiner (own firm with more than 25 employees)	0302/055/2
Shed builder (own firm with more than 25 employees)	0302/055/3
Cast concrete maker (own firm with more than 25 employees)	0302/055/4
Stonemason (own firm with more than 25 employees)	0302/094/5
Monumental mason (own firm with more than 25 employees)	0302/094/6
Builder and contractor (own firm with more than 25 employees)	0302/096/7
Painter and decorator (own firm with more than 25 employees)	0302/100/8
Earth-moving contractor (own firm, with more than 25 employees)	0302/104/9

Category 0303, employment status 1

Owner of small coalmine (with more than 25 employees)	0303/007/0
Ironstone mine owner (with more than 25 employees)	0303/009/1
Clay-pit owner (with more than 25 employees)	0303/009/2
Quarry owner (with more than 25 employees)	0303/009/3
Mineshaft sinker (own firm with more than 25 employees)	0303/009/4

Category 0304, employment status 1

Pottery maker (own firm with more than 25 employees)	0304/013/0
Foundryman (own foundry with more than 25 employees)	0304/020/1
Watchmaker and repairer (own firm with more than 25 employees)	0304/049/2
Goldsmith (own firm with more than 25 employees)	0304/051/3
Cabinet-maker (own firm with more than 25 employees)	0304/056/4
Tanner (own tannery with more than 25 employees)	0304/060/5
Hosiery maker (own firm with more than 25 employees)	0304/069/6
Tailor and outfitter (own firm with more than 25 employees)	0304/074/7
Baker (own bakery with more than 25 employees)	0304/078/8
Printer (own firm with more than 25 employees)	0304/087/9

Category 0401, employment status 1

Glue maker (own works with more than 25 employees)	0401/012/0
Scrapmetal merchant (with more than 25 employees)	0401/054/1
Screw maker (own works with more than 25 employees)	0401/054/2
Dressmaker (man, own business with more than 25 employees)	0401/076/3
Paint sprayer (own shop with more than 25 employees)	0401/099/4

Category 0402, employment status 1

Gravel-pit owner (with more than 25 employees)	0402/010/0
Quarry owner (with more than 25 employees)	0402/010/1
Slate maker (with more than 25 employees)	0402/010/2
Well borer (own firm with more than 25 employees)	0402/010/3
Opencast mine excavator (own firm with more than 25 employees)	0402/010/4

Category 0403, employment status 1

Demolition contractor (own firm with more than 25 employees)	0403/098/0
Steeple-jack (own firm with more than 25 employees)	0403/098/1
Asphalt layer (own firm with more than 25 employees)	0403/098/2
Roofing contractor (own firm with more than 25 employees)	0403/098/3
Drainage contractor (own firm with more than 25 employees)	0403/098/4

Category 0404, employment status 1

Gardening contractor (own firm with more than 25 employees)	0404/005/0
Warehouseman (own firm with more than 25 employees)	0404/136/1
Crate maker and packer (own firm with more than 25 employees)	0404/137/2
Credit inquiry agent (own firm with more than 25 employees)	0404/146/3
Dry-cleaner and launderer (own business with more than 25 employees)	0404/168/4

Category 0501, employment status 1

Docker (own gang with more than 25 men)	0501/133/0
Office cleaning contractor (own firm with more than 25 employees)	0501/166/1
Window cleaning contractor (own firm with more than 25 employees)	0501/166/2
Industrial cleaning contractor (own firm with more than 25 employees)	0501/166/3
Domestic cleaner (own agency with more than 25 employees)	0501/166/4

Title	Reference number
Category 0601, employment status 4	
Diplomat	0601/173/0
Member of Parliament	0601/173/1
Cabinet Minister	0601/173/2
Manager of labour exchange	0601/173/3
Senior civil servant	0601/173/4
Category 0602, employment status 4	
Public relations executive (large firm)	0602/206/0
Managing editor (large publishing house	0602/206/1
Film director	0602/207/2
TV producer	0602/207/3
Manager in large commercial design firm	0602/208/4
Category 0603, employment status 4	
Manager in large stock-broking firm	0603/149/0
Deputy town clerk	0603/174/1
Clerk to rural district council	0603/174/2
Weights and measures inspector	0603/174/3
Principal youth employment officer	0603/174/4
Category 0604, employment status 4	
Captain of merchant ship	0604/115/0
Chief inspector (municipal bus service)	0604/123/1
Station master of large station	0604/123/2
Chief controller (British Rail)	0604/126/3
Ship's radio officer	0604/128/4
Category 0605, employment status 4	
Manager in large wholesale firm	0605/143/0
Manager in large dairy	0605/143/1
Manager in large insurance firm	0605/150/2
Sales manager in large firm	0605/179/3
Circulation manager on newspaper	0605/179/4
Category 0606, employment status 4	
Colliery engineer	0606/175/0
Plant manager in large firm	0606/175/1
Site manager (construction industry)	0606/176/2
Colliery manager	0606/177/3
Brewery manager	0606/177/4
Production manager (large factory)	0606/177/5
Textile mill manager	0606/177/6
Personnel manager	0606/178/7
Manager of large drawing office in engineering firm	0606/218/8
Work study manager	0606/220/9
Category 0607, employment status 4	
Accounts manager	0607/138/0
Office manager (large commercial firm)	0607/138/1
Manager in large accountancy firm	0607/138/2
Bus service manager	0607/180/3
Dock manager	0607/180/4
Shipping agent	0607/180/5
Bank manager (large branch office)	0607/180/6
Chief engineer with electricity board	0607/180/7
Telephone manager	0607/180/8
Water board superintendent	0607/180/9
Category 0608, employment status 4	
Manager of large hotel	0608/156/0
Superintendent of large children's home	0608/157/1

Title	Reference number
Catering manager	0608/159/2
Player-manager of football club	0608/169/3
Manager of large theatre	0608/171/4

Category 0609, employment status 4

Chief fire officer	0609/151/0
Fire protection officer (in large firm)	0609/151/1
Police inspector	0609/152/2
Manager of large nursing home	0609/183/3
Public health inspector	0609/190/4
Headmaster of large secondary school	0609/193/5
Principal of commercial college	0609/194/6
Chief Welfare officer	0609/215/7
Secretary of large professional association	0609/216/8
General secretary of large trade union	0609/216/9

Category 0701, employment status 4

Manager in large security firm	0701/153/0
Security manager in large industrial firm	0701/153/1
Chief security officer at prison	0701/153/2
Manager in large credit rating firm	0701/153/3
Inspector in works security force	0701/153/4

Category 0801, employment status 4

Park superintendent	0801/005/0
Warehouse manager	0801/136/1
Dispatch controller in large warehouse	0801/136/2
Chief storekeeper in large factory	0801/136/3
Manager in large dry-cleaning firm	0801/168/4

Category 0901, employment status 2

Public relations consultant (own firm with less than 25 employees)	0901/206/0
Scriptwriter (own agency, with less than 25 employees)	0901/206/1
Pop musician (own group)	0901/207/2
Commercial artist (own studio with less than 25 employees)	0901/208/3
Engraver (own shop with employees)	0901/208/4

Category 0902, employment status 2

Coach operator (own firm with less than 25 employees)	0902/123/0
Ironmonger (own shop with employees)	0902/143/1
Garage proprietor (with less than 25 employees)	0902/147/2
Landlord of public house (with employees)	0902/154/3
Hotel proprietor (with less than 25 employees)	0902/156/4

Category 0903, employment status 2

Stockbroker (own firm with less than 25 employees)	0903/149/0
Insurance broker (own firm with less than 25 employees)	0903/149/1
Mortgage agent (own firm with less than 25 employees)	0903/149/2
Owner of investment company (with less than 25 employees)	0903/149/3
Financier (partner in small firm)	0903/149/4

Category 1001, employment status 2

Debt collector (own firm with less than 25 employees)	1001/139/0
Photostat printer and copier (own firm with less than 25 employees)	1001/140/1
Estate agent (partner in firm with less than 25 employees)	1001/150/2
Publicity agent (own firm with less than 25 employees)	1001/150/3
Owner of advertising agency (with less than 25 employees)	1001/150/4
Travel agent (own firm with less than 25 employees)	1001/150/5
Night-club owner (with less than 25 employees)	1001/159/6
Café proprietor (with less than 25 employees)	1001/159/7
Amusement arcade proprietor (with less than 25 employees)	1001/171/8
Undertaker (own business with less than 25 employees)	1001/171/9

Title	Reference number
Category 1002, employment status 2	
Map maker (own business with less than 25 employees)	1002/218/0
Furniture designer (own business with less than 25 employees)	1002/218/1
Tool designer (own business with less than 25 employees)	1002/218/2
Engineering draughtsman (own firm with less than 25 employees)	1002/218/3
Technical illustrator (own business with less than 25 employees)	1002/218/4
Category 1101, employment status 2	
Clay-pit owner (with less than 25 employees)	1101/009/0
Plumber (own business with less than 25 employees)	1101/045/1
Heating engineer (own business with less than 25 employees)	1101/046/2
Joiner (own business with less than 25 employees)	1101/055/3
Stonemason (with less than 25 employees)	1101/094/4
Builder and decorator (own business with less than 25 employees)	1101/096/5
Painter and decorator (own business with less than 25 employees)	1101/100/6
French polisher (own business with less than 25 employees)	1101/100/7
Sign writer (own business with employees)	1101/100/8
Earth-moving contractor (with less than 25 employees)	1101/104/9
Category 1102, employment status 2	
Radio and TV engineer (own business with less than 25 employees)	1102/024/0
Electrician (own repair shop with employees)	1102/027/1
Electrical instrument maker (own firm with less than 25 employees)	1102/028/2
Neon sign maker (own business with less than 25 employees)	1102/028/3
Taxi owner (with less than 25 employees)	1102/121/4
Driving instructor (own school with less than 25 employees)	1102/121/5
Haulage contractor (own business with less than 25 employees)	1102/122/6
Pastrycook (own shop with employees)	1102/162/7
Gentleman's hairdresser (own salon with less than 25 employees)	1102/167/8
Horse-racing trainer (own stable with less than 25 employees)	1102/169/9
Category 1103, employment status 2	
Blacksmith and wrought-iron work (own shop with employees)	1103/021/0
Oxy-acetylene cutter and welder (own shop with less than 25 employees)	1103/036/1
Watch repairer (own shop with employees)	1103/049/2
Goldsmith (own shop with less than 25 employees)	1103/051/3
Cabinet-maker (own shop with less than 25 employees)	1103/056/4
Sawmill owner (with less than 25 employees)	1103/057/5
Shoe repairer (own shop with employees)	1103/061/6
Postcard manufacturer (own business with less than 25 employees)	1103/084/7
Priner (own business with less than 25 employees)	1103/087/8
Organ builder (own business with less than 25 employees)	1103/091/9
Category 1201, employment status 2	
Fishing-boat owner (with less than 25 employees)	1201/001/0
Well borer (own business with less than 25 employees)	1201/010/1
Nail maker (own business with less than 25 employees)	1201/047/2
Scrap breaker (own business with less than 25 employees)	1201/054/3
Shirt maker (own business with less than 25 employees)	1201/076/4
Pickle maker (own business with less than 25 employees)	1201/081/5
Button maker (own business with less than 25 employees)	1201/092/6
Toy maker (own business with less than 25 employees)	1201/092/7
Glazier (own business with less than 25 employees)	1201/098/8
Barge owner (with less than 25 employees)	1201/116/9
Category 1202, employment status 2	
Gardening contractor (with less than 25 employees)	1202/005/0
Warehouse owner (with less than 25 employees)	1202/136/1
Owner of bottling plant (with less than 25 employees)	1202/137/2
Inquiry agent (with less than 25 employees)	1202/153/3
Owner of security firm (with less than 25 employees)	1202/153/4

Title	Reference number
Category 1203, employment status 2	
Stall-holder in market (with employees)	1203/146/0
Rag and bone collector (with employees)	1203/146/1
Owner of mobile shop (with employees)	1203/146/2
Laundry owner (with less than 25 employees)	1203/168/3
Dry-cleaner (own business with less than 25 employees)	1203/168/4
Category 1301, employment status 2	
Tarmac layer (own business with less than 25 employees)	1301/114/0
Car washer and cleaner (own business with less than 25 employees)	1301/114/1
Docker (own gang with less than 25 men)	1301/133/2
Domestic cleaner (own business with less than 25 employees)	1301/166/3
Office cleaner (own business with less than 25 employees)	1301/166/4
Category 1401, employment status 5	
Managing editor (small publishing house)	1401/206/0
Sub-editor on local newspaper	1401/206/1
Stage manager at small repertory theatre	1401/207/2
Floor manager at ballroom	1401/207/3
Manager in small textile designing firm	1401/208/4
Category 1402, employment status 5	
Primary school headmaster	1402/193/0
Principal of small language school	1402/194/1
Manager of Government training centre	1402/194/2
Senior official of Red Cross	1402/215/3
Youth club secretary	1402/215/4
Category 1403, employment status 5	
Manager of workmen's hostel	1403/156/0
Manager of small hotel	1403/156/1
Canteen manager	1403/159/2
General secretary of small trade union	1403/216/3
Senior official of employers' association	1403/216/4
Category 1404, employment status 5	
Plant manager in small engineering firm	1404/175/0
Manager of small foundry	1404/175/1
General manager of small building firm	1404/176/2
Manager of small quarry	1404/177/3
Bank manager (small branch office)	1404/180/4
Garage manager	1404/180/5
Harbour master	1404/180/6
Superintendent of sewage works	1404/180/7
Manager of small drawing office in engineering firm	1404/218/8
Manager of small computing centre	1404/220/9
Category 1405, employment status 5	
Bar manager in hotel	1405/154/0
Youth-hostel warden	1405/157/1
Ballroom manager	1405/171/2
Baths manager	1405/171/3
Launderette manager	1405/171/4
Category 1406, employment status 5	
Box office manager	1406/138/0
Betting shop manager	1406/138/1
Office manager in small commercial firm	1406/138/2
Showroom manager at garage	1406/143/3
Bookshop manager	1406/143/4
Manager in small insurance broking firm	1406/149/5
Manager of building society branch office	1406/150/6

Title	Reference number
Manager of small holiday camp	1406/150/7
Manager of small travel agency	1406/150/8
Contracts manager in advertising firm	1406/179/9

Category 1407, employment status 5

Manager of small bottle-making plant	1407/015/0
Manager of small firm of electrical installers and fitters	1407/030/1
Manager of small tool-making firm	1407/040/2
Manager of small heating and ventilating firm	1407/046/3
Manager of small firm of instrument-makers	1407/050/4
Manager of small hosiery firm	1407/069/5
Manager of tailor's shop	1407/074/6
Manager of butcher's shop	1407/079/7
Manager of small printing firm	1407/087/8
Manager of small coach hire firm	1407/120/9

Category 1501, employment status 5

Manager of mobile shop	1501/146/0
Manager of market stall	1501/146/1
Security officer in retail store	1501/153/2
Working manager in small security firm	1501/153/3
Manager in small credit rating firm	1501/153/4

Category 1601, employment status 5

Skipper of fishing boat	1601/001/0
Working manager in small scrap metal firm	1601/054/1
Fish shop manager	1601/081/2
Packaging manager (small factory)	1601/136/3
Manager in laundry and dry-cleaning firm	1601/168/4

Category 1701, employment status 1, 2 and 3

Doctor (general practioner)	1701/181/0
Psycho-analyst (private practice)	1701/181/1
Doctor (ear, nose, and throat specialist with private practice)	1701/181/2
Doctor (heart specialist with private practice)	1701/181/3
Certified accountant (partner in firm)	1701/209/4
Chartered accountant (partner in firm)	1701/209/5
Tax consultant (partner in firm)	1701/209/6
Financial adviser	1701/209/7
Company secretary and director	1701/210/8
Barrister	1701/214/9

Catetory 1702, employment status 1, 2 and 3

Dentist (private practice	1702/182/0
Architect (partner in firm)	1702/212/1
Veterinary surgeon (vet)	1702/217/2
Translator (freelance)	1702/217/3
Industrial designer (freelance)	1702/217/4

Category 1703, employment status 1, 2 and 3

Dispensing chemist (own shop)	1703/184/0
Structural engineer (consultant, own firm)	1703/195/1
Salvage engineer (partner in firm)	1703/196/2
Marine engineer (partner in firm)	1703/196/3
Mechanical engineer (own firm)	1703/196/4
Heating and ventilating engineer (own firm)	1703/196/5
Electrical engineer (consultant, own firm)	1703/197/6
Electronics engineer (partner in firm	1703/198/7
Naval architect (partner in firm)	1703/201/8
Surveyor and valuer (own firm)	1703/211/9

Title	Reference number
Category 1704, employment status 1, 2 and 3	
Baptist minister	1704/213/0
Vicar	1704/213/1
Curate	1704/213/2
Methodist minister	1704/213/3
Roman Catholic priest	1704/213/4
Category 1801, employment status 7	
Doctor (specialist at hospital)	1801/181/0
Dentist	1801/182/1
Optician	1801/186/2
University lecturer	1801/192/3
Certified accountant (employed by local council)	1801/209/4
Chartered accountant (employed in industry)	1801/209/5
Company secretary	1801/210/6
Surveyor	1801/211/7
Judge	1801/214/8
Lawyer (employed by government department)	1801/214/9
Category 1802, employment status 7	
Borough engineer	1802/195/0
Aeronautical engineer	1802/196/1
Electrical engineer at power station	1802/197/2
Computer designer	1802/198/3
Production engineer	1802/200/4
Colliery surveyor	1802/201/5
Industrial chemist	1802/204/6
Physicist	1802/205/7
Town planner	1802/212/8
Librarian	1802/217/9
Category 1803, employment status 7	
Captain in Salvation Army	1803/213/0
Chaplain in armed forces	1803/213/1
Missionary	1803/213/2
Bishop	1803/213/3
Rabbi	1803/213/4
Category 1901, employment status 6 and 7	
Editorial assistant in publishing house	1901/206/0
Leader writer on newspaper	1901/206/1
Public relations officer	1901/206/2
Newspaper reporter	1901/206/3
Musician in orchestra	1901/207/4
Actor in repertory theatre	1901/207/5
Radio announcer	1901/207/6
Advertising designer	1901/208/7
Window dresser (man)	1901/208/8
Picture cleaner and restorer	1901/208/9
Category 1902, employment status 7	
Local trade union official (full time)	1902/216/0
Conservative Party agent	1902/216/1
Labour Party agent	1902/216/2
Research officer of employers' association	1902/216/3
Research officer in trade union	1902/216/4
Category 1903, employment status 6 and 7	
Work study engineer	1903/199/0
Laboratory assistant	1903/219/1
Laboratory superintendent	1903/219/2

Title	Reference number
Medical technician	1903/219/3
Computer programmer	1903/220/4

Category 1904, employment status 6 and 7

Collector of taxes	1904/142/0
X-ray operator	1904/185/1
Physiotherapist	1904/188/2
Occupational therapist	1904/189/3
Sanitary inspector	1904/190/4
Secondary school master	1904/193/5
Grammar school master	1904/193/6
Dancing instructor (man)	1904/194/7
Training officer in large firm	1904/194/8
Social welfare worker (man)	1904/215/9

Category 1905, employment status 6

Foreman at coal merchants	1905/123/0
Goods foreman (British Rail)	1905/123/1
Bus inspector	1905/123/2
Goods inspector (British Rail)	1905/123/3
Platform inspector (British Rail)	1905/123/4

Category 1906, employment status 7

Flight engineer (civil airline)	1906/117/0
Instructor at flying school	1906/117/1
Aircraft navigator (civil airline)	1906/117/2
Airline pilot	1906/117/3
Test pilot	1906/117/4

Category 2001, employment status 1 and 2

Chiropodist (own practice, with employees)	2001/187/0
Physiotherapist (own practice, with employees)	2001/188/1
Masseur (own practice, with employees)	2001/191/2
Herbalist (own shop with employees)	2001/191/3
Headmaster and owner of private school	2001/193/4
Dancing instructor (own school with employees)	2001/194/5
Head and owner of secretarial college	2001/194/6
Riding instructor (own school with employees)	2001/194/7
Riding instructor (own school with employees)	2001/194/7
Industrial consultant (own firm with employees)	2001/199/8
Computer consultant (own firm with employees)	2001/220/9

Category 2101, employment status 3

Author	2101/206/0
Freelance journalist	2101/206/1
TV actor	2101/207/2
Comedian (TV and theatre)	2101/207/3
Opera singer	2101/207/4
Circus artist (man)	2101/207/5
Portrait painter	2101/208/6
Interior decorator (freelance)	2101/208/7
Stage designer (freelance)	2101/208/8
Commercial artist (freelance)	2101/208/9

Category 2102, employment status 3

Chiropodist (own practice)	2102/187/0
Physiotherapist (own practice)	2102/188/1
Osteopath (own practice)	2102/191/2
Language teacher (freelance)	2102/194/3
Work study consultant (freelance)	2102/199/4

Title	Reference number
Category 2201, employment status 6	
Chief traffic inspector (Post Office)	2201/126/0
Chief supervisor (Post Office)	2201/127/1
Chief supervisor at telephone exchange	2201/127/2
Supervisor of telegraph services (Post Office)	2201/128/3
Police sergeant	2201/152/4
Category 2202, employment status 6	
Supervisor in postal sorting office	2202/139/0
Duty officer at airport	2202/139/1
Chief cashier	2202/139/2
Chief clerk	2202/139/3
Medical records officer (at hospital)	2202/139/4
Office supervisor	2202/139/5
Chief book-keeper	2202/139/6
Typing pool superintendent (man)	2202/141/7
Chief draughtsman	2202/218/8
Section leader in technical drawing office	2202/218/9
Category 2203, employment status 6	
Supervisor in large store	2203/144/0
Inspector in insurance company	2203/150/1
Chief warder (at prison)	2203/153/2
Head porter at hotel	2203/172/3
Baths superintendent	2203/172/4
Category 2301, employment status 7	
Train controller (British Rail)	2301/126/0
Flight controller at airport	2301/126/1
Radio operator on ship	2301/128/2
Police constable	2301/152/3
Police officer (CID)	2301/152/4
Category 2302, employment status 7	
Engineering draughtsman	2302/218/0
Draughtsman	2302/218/1
Technical illustrator	2302/218/2
Tracer in drawing office	2302/218/3
Map drawer and colourer	2302/218/4
Category 2303, employment status 7	
Library assistant	2303/139/0
Cashier	2303/139/1
Records clerk	2303/139/2
Audit clerk	2303/139/3
Electric meter reader	2303/139/4
Youth employment officer	2303/139/5
Sales representative	2303/148/6
Commercial traveller	2303/148/7
Insurance collector	2303/150/8
Travel agency employee	2303/150/9
Category 2304, employment status 7	
Computer assistant	2304/140/0
Private secretary (man)	2304/141/1
Shorthand writer (man)	2304/141/2
Bookshop assistant (man)	2304/144/3
Shoe shop assistant (man)	2304/144/4
Salesman at gentlemen's outfitter	2304/144/5
Car salesman	2304/144/6
Grocer's shop assistant	2304/144/7

Title	Reference number
Jeweller's shop assistant	2304/144/8
Newspaper kiosk attendant (man)	2304/144/9

Category 2401, employment status 7

Switchboard operator (man)	2401/127/0
Telephone operator (man)	2401/127/1
Ice cream seller	2401/146/2
Vacuum cleaner salesman	2401/146/3
Newspaper seller	2401/146/4
Bank guard	2401/153/5
Car park attendant	2401/153/6
Store detective	2401/153/7
Traffic warden	2401/153/8
Night watchman	2401/153/9

Category 2402, employment status 7

Cloakroom attendant (man)	2402/172/0
Recording engineer	2402/172/1
Cinema projectionist	2402/172/2
Press photograher	2402/172/3
Porter and liftman at hotel	2402/172/4
Bill sticker	2402/172/5
Male model	2402/172/6
Doorman	2402/172/7
Courier for travel agency	2402/172/8
Baths attendant	2402/172/9

Category 2501, employment status 6 and 7

House father in children's home	2501/157/0
Hostel supervisor	2501/157/1
Hotel inspector	2501/157/2
Lodging house supervisor	2501/157/3
Mountain rescue station instructor	2501/157/4

Category 2601, employment status 6

Sports club steward	2601/155/0
Chief steward on dining car (British Rail)	2601/160/1
Head waiter	2601/160/2
Canteen supervisor	2601/161/3
Butler	2601/164/4

Category 2801, employment status 6 and 7

Grill hand (at restaurant)	2801/162/0
Chef	2801/162/1
Pastry cook (at hotel)	2801/162/2
Ladies hairdresser (man)	2801/167/3
Gentleman's hairdresser	2801/167/4

Category 2901, employment status 7

Barman	2901/155/0
Steward at working men's club	2901/155/1
Dining car attendant (British Rail)	2901/160/2
Waiter	2901/160/3
Snack bar attendant	2901/161/4
Table clearer at cafeteria (man)	2901/161/5
Sleeping car attendant (British Rail)	2901/164/6
Footman at large house	2901/164/7
Shoe black	2901/164/8
Cabin steward (civil airline)	2901/164/9

Category 3001, employment status 6

Supervisor in watch repair shop	3001/049/0
Foreman in firm making scientific instruments	3001/050/1

Title	Reference number
Foreman in furniture-making firm	3001/056/2
Foreman in textile-printing firm	3001/086/3
Foreman in printing firm	3001/088/4

Category 3002, employment status 6

Foreman in machine shop	3002/038/0
Tool room foreman	3002/040/1
Assistant engineer at coal mine	3002/042/2
Maintenance foreman at factory	3002/042/3
Foreman fitter	3002/043/4
Maintenance foreman at engine sheds	3002/043/5
Quality control foreman	3002/053/6
Carriage inspector (British Rail)	3002/053/7
Foreman joiner	3002/055/8
Foreman at sports goods manufacturers	3002/091/9

Category 3003, employment status 6

Assistant engineer (Post Office)	3003/025/0
Maintenance foreman (Post Office)	3003/025/1
Foreman ganger (British Rail)	3003/026/2
Power station foreman	3003/027/3
Foreman in electronics factory	3003/028/4
Garage foreman	3003/041/5
Gas Board foreman	3003/045/6
Water Board inspector	3003/045/7
Dock foreman	3003/133/8
Fire prevention officer at factory	3003/151/9

Category 3004, employment status 6

Foreman at gasworks	3004/011/0
Foreman at pottery kiln	3004/015/1
Blast furnance foreman	3004/018/2
Shipyard foreman	3004/035/3
Foreman welder	3004/036/4
Foreman in electro-plating plant	3004/044/5
Foreman in wagon repair shop	3004/052/6
Sawmill foreman	3004/057/7
Foreman in boot and shoe factory	3004/061/8
Foreman in water pumping station	3004/105/9

Category 3005, employment status 6

Foreman in paint factory	3005/012/0
Brickyard foreman	3005/013/1
Yard foreman at tannery	3005/060/2
Weaving foreman in woollen mill	3005/068/3
Foreman in clothes manufacturing firm	3005/074/4
Brewery foreman	3005/080/5
Dairy foreman	3005/081/6
Foreman in cigarette factory	3005/082/7
Waterworks foreman	3005/092/8
Foreman at local refuse tip	3005/114/9

Category 3006, employment status 6

Foreman in landscape gardening firm	3006/005/0
Mate on barge-boat	3006/116/1
Petty officer on passenger ship	3006/116/2
Head postman	3006/129/3
Ticket inspector (British Rail)	3006/132/4
Timber-yard foreman	3006/136/5
Warehouse foreman	3006/136/6
Laundry foreman	3006/168/7

Title	Reference number
Head porter in hospital	3006/170/8
Supervisor in ambulance service	3006/170/9

Category 3007, employment status 6

Mate on fishing boat	3007/001/0
Haulage foreman at coal mine	3007/007/1
Deputy at coal mine (underground supervisor)	3007/007/2
Training officer at coal mine	3007/008/3
Foreman at stone quarry	3007/010/4

Category 3008, employment status 6

Foreman in engineering construction firm	3008/034/0
Building site foreman	3008/098/1
Ganger (road repair work)	3008/098/2
Inspector of drainage (local government employee)	3008/098/3
Foreman in excavation firm	3008/104/4

Category 3101, employment status 7

Watch repairer	3101/049/0
Clock maker	3101/049/1
Camera mechanic	3101/050/2
Typewriter mechanic	3101/050/3
Microscope maker	3101/050/4
Jewellery maker	3101/051/5
Jewellery engraver	3101/051/6
Furniture repairer	3101/056/7
Compositor	3101/085/8
Type-setter	3101/085/9

Category 3102, employment status 7

BBC engineer	3102/024/0
Television installer	3102/024/1
X-ray engineer	3102/024/2
Radio and TV repairman	3102/024/3
Television studio technician	3102/024/4

Category 3103, employment status 7

Gas fitter	3103/045/0
Builder's joiner	3103/055/1
Kiln repairer	3103/093/2
Tiler and plasterer	3103/093/3
Slate cutter	3103/094/4
Stone cutter	3103/094/5
Clerk of works	3103/096/6
Paint-shop worker	3103/100/7
House painter	3103/100/8
Furniture polisher	3103/100/9

Category 3104, employment status 7

Post Office engineer	3104/025/0
Electricity Board maintenance man	3104/027/1
Electronic fitter	3104/028/2
Garage mechanic	3104/041/3
Fire brigade man	3104/151/4

Category 3105, employment status 7

Professional cricketer	3105/169/0
Professional footballer	3105/169/1
Golf club professional	3105/169/2
Swimming instructor	3105/169/3
Football coach	3105/169/4

Title	Reference number
Category 3106, employment status 7	
Welder	3106/036/0
Lathe operator	3106/037/1
Tool maker	3106/040/2
Maintenance fitter at engineering factory	3106/042/3
Aircraft fitter	3106/043/4
Wagon maker and repairer	3106/052/5
Dental mechanic	3106/091/6
Carpet fitter	3106/091/6
Musical instrument maker	3106/091/8
Artificial limb maker	3106/091/9
Category 3107, employment status 7	
Clay moulder in pottery	3107/013/0
Glass blower	3107/014/1
Pottery decorator	3107/016/2
Lead pipe maker	3107/019/3
Sheet metal worker	3107/033/4
Coppersmith	3107/033/5
Boilermaker	3107/035/6
Riveter at shipyard	3107/035/7
Lathe operator and setter	3107/038/8
Printing-press operator	3107/086/9
Category 3108, employment status 7	
Telephone line maintenance worker	3108/026/0
Driver of diesel engine (British Rail)	3108/118/1
Shunter (British Rail)	3108/124/2
Signalman (British Rail)	3108/125/3
Level-crossing keeper	3108/125/4
Category 3109, employment status 7	
Coalminer (face worker)	3109/007/0
Coalminer (maintenance worker)	3109/007/1
Clay-pit worker (underground)	3109/009/2
Ironstone mine worker	3109/009/3
Tunneller	3109/009/4
Category 3110, employment status 7	
Steelwork erector	3110/034/0
Winding engineman (at coalmine)	3110/103/1
Swing-bridge operator	3110/103/2
Bulldozer driver	3110/104/3
Excavator operator	3110/104/4
Category 3111, employment status 7	
Kiln worker (pottery-making)	3111/015/0
Blast furnaceman	3111/018/1
Forge worker	3111/021/2
Shopfitter	3111/059/3
Saddler and leather worker	3111/063/4
Tailor's cutter	3111/077/5
Ovenman at bakery	3111/078/6
Vatman at brewery	3111/080/7
Colour printer	3111/088/8
Engine house attendant (at factory)	3111/105/9
Category 3112, employment status 7	
Railway guard	3112/119/0
Coach tour driver	3112/120/1
Chauffeur	3112/121/2

Title	Reference number
Delivery van driver	3112/122/3
Long-distance lorry driver	3112/122/4
Category 3201, employment status 7	
Machinist in pottery factory	3201/017/0
Assembler in factory making electrical goods	3201/029/1
Machinist (engineering factory)	3201/039/2
Instrument tester (engineering factory)	3201/053/3
Car assembly line worker	3201/054/4
Woollen mill operative	3201/066/5
Machine operative in chocolate factory	3201/081/6
Machine operative in tobacco factory	3201/082/7
Pain sprayer (car factory)	3201/099/8
Boiler-room attendant	3201/102/9
Category 3202, employment status 7	
Bricklayer's labourer	3202/097/0
Stonemason's labourer	3202/097/1
Asphalter	3202/098/2
Demolition worker	3202/098/3
Scaffolding erector	3202/098/4
Water Board fitter	3202/098/5
Maintenance handyman	3202/098/6
Property repairer	3202/098/7
Concrete layer	3202/098/8
Road mender	3202/098/9
Category 3203, employment status 7	
Deckhand on fishing trawler	3203/001/0
Engine room hand on fishing trawler	3203/001/1
Surface worker at coal mine	3203/008/2
Brick-field worker	3203/010/3
Quarry worker	3203/010/4
Category 3204, employment status 7	
Groundsman	3204/005/0
Track maintenance worker (British Rail)	3204/106/1
Deckhand (Merchant ship)	3204/116/2
Post Office sorter	3204/129/3
Bus conductor	3204/131/4
Lock-keeper	3204/135/5
Warehouse porter	3204/136/6
Milk roundsman	3204/145/7
Laundry worker	3204/168/8
Ambulance man	3204/170/9
Category 3301, employment status 7	
Coal heaver at docks	3301/133/0
Dock labourer	3301/133/1
Cargo inspector at docks	3301/133/2
Shedman at docks	3301/133/3
Fish dock porter	3301/133/4
Category 3302, employment status 7	
General labourer (engineering factory)	3302/108/0
Gasworks labourer	3302/111/1
Navvy	3302/113/2
Factory cleaner (man)	3302/114/3
Furniture remover	3302/114/4
Factory messenger	3302/130/5
Ticket collector (British Rail)	3302/132/6

Title	Reference number
Railway goods yard worker	3302/132/7
Lorry driver's mate	3302/134/8
Kitchen porter	3302/163/9

Category 3401, employment status 3

Owner and skipper of pleasure launch	3401/115/0
Ferryman (own boat)	3401/115/1
Owner and Pilot of charter plane	3401/117/2
Flying instructor (freelance)	3401/117/3
Owner and pilot of plane giving pleasure flights	3401/117/4

Category 3402, employment status 3

Filling station owner (no employees)	3402/147/0
Taxi and garage owner (no employees)	3402/147/1
Innkeeper	3402/154/2
Landlord of public house	3402/154/3
Licensed victualler	3402/154/4

Category 3403, employment status 3

Confectioner (own shop)	3403/143/0
Pig dealer	3403/143/1
Off-licensee	3403/143/2
Second-hand car dealer	3403/143/3
Lodging house proprietor	3403/156/4

Category 3501, employment status 3

Football pools agent	3501/150/0
Insurance agent	3501/150/1
Fish-and-chip shop owner	3501/159/2
Snack bar owner	3501/159/3
Bookmaker	3501/171/4
Professional gambler	3501/171/5
Fortune teller	3501/171/6
Stall-holder at fairground	3501/171/7
Portrait photograher	3501/171/8
Street photographer	3501/171/9

Category 3502, employment status 3

Rent collector (self-employed)	3502/139/0
Commercial traveller (working on commission)	3502/148/1
Furniture designer (freelance)	3502/218/2
Graphic designer (freelance)	3502/218/3
Technical illustrator (freelance)	3502/218/4

Category 3601, employment status 3

Professional boxer	3601/169/0
Tennis coach (freelance)	3601/169/1
Jockey	3601/169/2
Professional wrestler	3601/169/3
Racing driver	3601/169/4

Category 3602, employment status 3

Radio and TV repairer (self-employed)	3602/024/0
Electrical wirer (self-employed)	3602/027/1
Electrical appliance repairer (self-employed)	3602/028/2
Motor mechanic (self-employed)	3602/041/3
Typewriter repairer (self-employed)	3602/050/4
Jewellery designer (freelance)	3602/051/5
Furniture restorer (self-employed)	3602/056/6
Antique restorer (self-employed)	3602/056/7
Wig maker (own shop)	3602/167/8
Barber (own shop)	3602/167/9

Title	Reference number
Category 3603, employment status 3	
Garden furniture maker (self-employed)	3603/055/0
Floor layer (self-employed)	3603/093/1
Architectural model maker (self-employed)	3603/095/2
House painter (self-employed)	3603/100/3
Paper hanger (self-employed)	3603/100/4
Category 3604, employment status 3	
Pottery decorator (self-employed)	3604/016/0
Cycle repairer (self-employed)	3604/043/1
Wood carver (self-employed)	3604/059/2
Bespoke tailor (self-employed)	3604/074/3
Tripe dresser and seller (self-employed)	3604/079/4
Bookbinder (self-employed)	3604/088/5
Photographic engraver (self-employed)	3604/088/6
Basket maker (self-employed)	3604/091/7
Piano tuner (self-employed)	3604/091/8
Sports equipment repairer (self-employed)	3604/091/9
Category 3605, employment status 3	
Taxi owner-driver	3605/121/0
Driving instructor (freelance)	3605/121/1
Van man and carrier (self-employed)	3605/122/2
Cattle transporter (self-employed)	3605/122/3
Sandwich maker and seller (self-employed)	3605/162/4
Category 3606, employment status 3	
Saw sharpener and repairer (self-employed)	3606/048/0
Key cutter (self-employed)	3606/048/1
Knife and scissors grinder (self-employed)	3606/048/2
Fellmonger (self-employed)	3606/060/3
Hand weaver (self-employed)	3606/068/4
Category 3701, employment status 3	
Fisherman (self-employed, own boat)	3701/001/0
Lobster boat man (own boat)	3701/001/1
Shellfish gatherer and seller (own business)	3701/001/2
Stone sett maker (self-employed)	3701/010/3
Stone-dresser (self-employed)	3701/098/4
Category 3702, employment status 3	
Charcoal burner (self-employed)	3702/012/0
Curtain maker (self-employed)	3702/076/1
Tapestry restorer (self-employed)	3702/076/2
Cheese maker (self-employed)	3702/081/3
Toffee maker (self-employed)	3702/081/4
Category 3703, employment status 3	
Jobbing gardener	3703/005/0
Market trader	3703/146/1
Barrow boy	3703/146/2
Hawker	3703/146/3
Newspaper seller (self-employed)	3703/146/4
Category 3801, employment status 3	
Odd job man (self-employed)	3801/114/0
Parcel carrier (self-employed)	3801/130/1
Chimney sweep (self-employed)	3801/166/2
Window cleaner (self-employed)	3801/166/3
Office cleaner (man, self-employed)	3801/166/4

Title	Reference number
Category 3901, employment status 1, 2, 4 and 5	
Farm agent	3901/002/0
Farmer (large farm with more than 25 employees)	3901/002/1
Farm bailiff	3901/002/2
Poultry farmer (own business with less than 25 employees)	3901/002/3
Market gardener (own business with less than 25 employees)	3901/002/4
Proprietor of riding school	3901/002/5
Owner of agricultural machinery hire firm	3901/004/6
Owner of pest control firm	3901/004/7
Forestry manager	3901/006/8
District officer in Forestry Commission	3901/006/9
Category 4001, employment status 3	
Beekeeper	4001/002/0
Nurseryman (own gardens)	4001/002/1
Small holder	4001/002/2
Pig keeper	4001/002/3
Dog breeder	4001/002/4
Category 4002, employment status 3	
Mole catcher	4002/003/0
Hedger and ditcher (self-employed)	4002/003/1
Turf cutter (self-employed)	4002/003/2
Peat cutter (self-employed)	4002/006/3
Tree surgeon (self-employed)	4002/006/4
Category 4101, employment status 6	
Supervisor at poultry farm	4101/003/0
Farm foreman	4101/003/1
Head keeper at zoo	4101/003/2
Forester	4101/006/3
Forestry Commission warden	4101/006/4
Category 4201, employment status 7	
Gardener at bulb and seed farm	4201/003/0
Cowman	4201/003/1
Fruit farm worker	4201/003/2
Pest control inspector	4201/003/3
Zoo keeper	4201/003/4
Market gardener (employee)	4201/003/5
Shepherd	4201/003/6
Tractor driver and mechanic	4201/004/7
Tree planter	4201/006/8
Tree feller	4201/006/9
Category 4301, employment status 4	
Senior naval officer	4301/221/0
Junior naval officer	4301/221/1
RAF officer	4301/221/2
Senior army officer	4301/221/3
Junior army officer	4301/221/4
Category 4401, employment status 6	
Petty officer in navy	4401/221/0
Army sergeant	4401/221/1
Army corporal	4401/221/2
RAF sergeant	4401/221/3
RAF corporal	4401/221/4
Category 4501, employment status 7	
Ordinary seaman, navy	4501/221/0
Able seaman, navy	4501/221/1

Title	Reference number
Army private	4501/221/2
RAF aircraftman, second class	4501/221/3
RAF leading aircraftman	4501/221/4

(1) All titles selected should be titles likely to be known to the great majority of respondents in a national sample. (By following this rule it may be supposed that, by and large, we did in fact favour the more commonly occurring occupations.)

(2) Subject to meeting the requirement stated in (1), the titles selected should cover the range of occupations comprised by the category, taking into account all occupational attributes known to be regularly associated with assessments of 'general desirability'. (In accordance with this rule, we were alert to possible heterogeneity among the sets of occupations making up the different occupation grading units within a category. But it was by no means the case that representative titles were always distributed equally between grading units or even that each grading unit provided at least one title. For example, it sometimes appeared that most of the heterogeneity among the occupations covered by a category as a whole was concentrated within a single grading unit—from which most titles would then of course be taken.)

(3) Where rule (1) allowed, and rule (2) made it desirable, ten occupation titles were selected from each category; otherwise, five titles were selected.

Proceeding in this manner, we were able to produce sets of representative titles for all our categories except one. This was a category (2701 in Table 6.2) made up of a single occupation grading unit and covering domestic housekeepers with the status of employee. In this case, we were unable to find any occupations falling within the category which were typically engaged in by males. We decided therefore that this category should be excluded from our scale.

Of the remaining 124 categories, 48 were represented by 10 titles and 76 by 5 titles, giving a total number of titles for empirical grading of 860. Table 4.2 lists these titles in category order. The reference number of a representative title is that of its occupation grading unit (see above, p. 27) plus an eighth digit of from 0 to 4 or 0 to 9 which signifies its (arbitrary) position in the category. It may be noted that titles often include an explicit indication of employment status. It was our policy to give such an indication in all cases other than where employment status was evident enough without it,* or where the status was that simply of 'employee' (i.e. code 7 in Table 4.1).

The grading task and problems of commensuration

Having determined the categories of our scale and selected representative titles from categories for the purpose of securing empirical gradings, the next

* In the case of occupations of 'employer' or 'manager' status, it will be seen that we did not always spell out the number of employees in full. Sometimes it appeared sufficient to indicate simply that the enterprise in which a man worked was 'large' or 'small'.

question to be considered was that of the form of the grading exercise that respondents in our inquiry should be asked to carry out.

There are two assumptions that one can make about the mental process involved in assessing occupations according to their 'social standing' or any such characteristic. One is that respondents in effect have a scale in their heads and assign occupations to positions along it discretely, without making explicit comparisons among occupations. The other is that assessment is a comparative activity and that judgements are usually of relative position. The former assumption implies that the assessment is intrinsically a *rating* activity, while the latter implies that it is a process of ordering or *ranking*. In the absence of any decisive empirical evidence, we inclined to the common-sense view that, whatever may be the nature of the process by which very disparate occupations are judged, when it is a question of grading a number of occupations some of which may have broadly similar attributes, judgement will be facilitated and refined if comparisons between occupations can readily be made. In practice, therefore, we favoured a grading task which would require a respondent to *rank* occupation titles, in an order corresponding to his view of their 'social standing'.

However, while this method might be thought preferable in terms of psychological validity, it had to be recognized that it gave rise to two particular difficulties. First, the number of occupation titles that a respondent could be expected to handle in a ranking task would be less than in a rating task, since in the latter he would be required simply to give a score on, say, a seven-point scale to each title presented to him. Thus a ranking task would demand *ceteris paribus* a larger sample of respondents. Secondly, and more seriously, where respondents are not all grading the same set of occupations—as clearly they cannot be in a study in which gradings for 860 titles are required—the rank orderings produced by different respondents cannot be taken as directly comparable in the way that numerical ratings might be. It is probable that the grading distributions of respondents will differ because of differences in the subsets of occupations ranked. We were then faced with the need to find a procedure by which the gradings of different respondents could be rendered commensurate.

Various procedures suggested themselves as possible solutions to this problem, and there were no decisive *a priori* reasons for preferring any one of the possibilities. We decided to take the solution which seemed to be the safest, to undertake a preliminary exploration of its effectiveness and, if the assessments which it produced reached an acceptable level of reliability, to employ it in the main study without troubling ourselves with a search for marginal improvements by the use of rival methods.

This solution was to arrange that every respondent in the empirical grading study should begin his or her task by ranking according to their 'social standing' a set of 20 *standard* occupation titles which were not included in the 860 representative titles. After the respondent had assured the interviewer that he was quite happy with the ordering of the standard occupations, he would then be given a further set of 20 cards, each bearing the title of one of the 860 representative titles, and be asked to insert each of these into the ranking of the standard occupations at the point at which, in terms of its 'social standing', he believed it belonged. Respondents would be informed that they could tie one or more representative occupation titles with a standard occupation title (or with several titles, if these had been tied in the preliminary grading) by placing them alongside the standard title; that they could place one or more ranks (i.e. single cards or tied sets of cards) of representative titles between two neighbouring ranks of standard titles; and that they could place one or more ranks of representative titles above the topmost standard title or below the lowest standard title.* In this way, some common basis for the ranking and the scoring of the representative titles could be secured.

Before employing this procedure it was, however, necessary to subject it to practical trial, in particular to ascertain whether the selection of the common set of 20 standard occupations was in any degree critical. To this end we carried out a small pilot study in which the procedure was the reverse of that proposed for the main study. Here we used a *single* set of 20 dummy 'representative' titles which did not vary from respondent to respondent, but we employed *two* sets (A and B) of standard occupations, each constructed to span the whole range of 'social standing' in a fairly regular fashion. A quota sample of 50 respondents, drawn from the population of the London area, was split by a randomizing procedure into two equal sub-samples. Members of one sub-sample first graded the standard occupations of set A and then interpolated the dummy representative titles into their grading distribution; members of the other sample first graded the standard occupations of set B and then interpolated the same dummy representative titles as the first sample into their grading distribution. In the first place, this exercise confirmed that respondents found no noticeable difficulty in performing the grading task which we planned for our main national inquiry. Furthermore, the analysis of the data obtained (which is reported in Appendix B, 'The London Inquiry') strongly suggested that the scoring of representative titles in the context of one set of standard titles does not differ from the scoring of the same titles in the context of another set of standard titles—in other words, choice of standard titles for purposes of commensuration is not critical.

For the purpose of the main grading inquiry, therefore, we adopted a single standard set of 20 occupation titles constituted by selection from among the 40 standard titles employed in the London inquiry. We drew on the evidence of this study to enable us to cover the range of 'social standing' in as regular a manner as possible, and also to assist in the selection of titles with relatively low standard errors of grading (i.e. little respondent disagreement). The 20 standard titles employed in the main inquiry are listed in Table 4.3.

Allocation of grading tasks to respondents

As we indicated above, the selection of either ten or five titles from each of our 124 categories produced a total of 860 representative titles for empirical

---

* See the instructions to interviewers for the empirical grading inquiry given in Appendix D.

TABLE 4.3

The twenty standard titles which were graded initially
by all respondents in the main grading inquiry

1 Auctioneer and valuer (own business with less than 25 employees)
2 Bricklayer
3 Building site labourer
4 Bus driver
5 Business manager (large commercial firm)
6 Butcher (own shop with employees)
7 Carpenter
8 Civil engineer
9 Crane operator
10 Foreman (engineering factory)
11 Male nurse
12 Postman
13 Primary school teacher (man)
14 Printer (own business, no employees)
15 Process worker (chemical industry)
16 Radar mechanic
17 Railway porter
18 Shoe repairer (own shop, no employees)
19 Solicitor
20 Upholsterer

grading in our main inquiry. The grading task described in the preceding section demands that each respondent should grade 20 respresentative titles, in addition to the 20 standard titles of Table 4.3. In the absence of information on the ratio of (a) the variance of occupation titles within categories to (b) the variance of respondents grading the same title, we decided, in accordance with the reasoning set out on p. 21 above, to ensure that the scale value for each category, i.e. the category mean, should be derived from a constant number of gradings, irrespective of the number of titles in a category. In the light of the reliability estimate obtained in the London inquiry (see Appendix B, p. 170) we settled on 100 gradings per category, giving us ten gradings for titles in a ten-title category and twenty for titles in a five-title category. Since we required 124 × 100 gradings, and since each respondent was to supply 20, this meant that we required 620 respondents.

A special-purpose computer program was written to generate the 620 schedules on which the interviewers were to record the respondents' gradings. Schedules were individually numbered from 1 to 620 because every schedule was different from every other schedule, and every one of the 620 had to be satisfactorily completed. The schedules were output on the line-printer of the computer. Every eighth schedule was printed a second time (with an indication that it was a duplicate) for use in a repeat interview, to be undertaken in order to investigate the extent of respondent inconsistency (see above p. 21).

The first sheet of a schedule was a protocol in which the usual basic information about a respondent was to be inserted. The remaining sheets contained a list of forty occupation titles in alphabetical order, with space for a grade to be inserted against each title by the interviewer. Twenty of the titles were the titles of the standard occupations and these appeared on every schedule, though in a position which varied with the initial letters of the other twenty titles (all forty being in alphabetical order). A record was kept on magnetic tape of the contents of every schedule, and markers were retained to ensure precise matching of schedules with the data obtained in the empirical inquiry.

In randomly sampling representative occupations for assignment to a particular schedule, care was taken to ensure that the same title was never assigned more than once to that schedule. In order to keep the number of assignments of a particular occupation as close as possible to the desired figure of ten (for occupations in ten-title categories) or twenty (for occupations in five-title categories) an embargo was set on drawing an occupation more than its allotted ten or twenty times. Towards the end of the sampling task, as the computer was working on the production of schedule number 617, this embargo was relaxed because the random number generator was being entered more than a specified number of times in order to find one extra title which was available for assignment and had not already been assigned to the current schedule. 804 of the 860 representative titles were assigned exactly ten or exactly twenty times.*

The representative titles were typed in upper-case pica type and printed by a photographic process on to 25 × 88 mm pieces of white card. The standard occupations were produced by the same process on to pieces of blue card. In making up an envelope of interview materials for a respondent the requisite pack of cards was assembled by reference to the titles printed on the schedule by the computer. Six pink specimen cards bearing dummy titles, which were to be used by the interviewer to demonstrate the grading task, were issued to each interviewer.

The sample

The design of the enquiry was such that all 620 schedules had to be completed, together with as many as possible of the one-in-eight duplicate schedules. The population which we wished to sample was the population of males and females in England and Wales who were aged 20–64 inclusive. Details of the sample design are given in Appendix C. It may be summarily described as a self-weighting random sample drawn from two polling districts in each of thirty parliamentary constituencies in England and Wales. The sampling frame was the electoral

---

* One of the 56 exceptions is the very last occupation in the list which, owing to a defect in the stipulation of initial probabilities, was assigned only 4 times. This of course accounts for some of the over-assignments of other occupations. After careful consideration it was decided that we could not justify the considerable expenditure of computing time which would be involved in re-running the assignment program in order to eliminate this irritating but wholly inconsequential blemish. Nor did we feel justified in taking the risk of interfering with the complex automatic recording and printing process by attempting to reallocate the 860th occupation by hand.

registers compiled in October 1970 but interviewing did not take place until April/May of 1972, by which time the registers were nineteen months old.

Conduct of the interviewing

Interviewing for the inquiry was undertaken by a commercial agency, the British Market Research Bureau.* We ourselves took a leading part in training the interviewers in the administration of the grading task.

The written instructions given to interviewers are reproduced in full in Appendix D. The interviewer began by using the pink specimen cards to demonstrate the task, showing how occupations were to be ranked in order of their 'social standing', and indicating that ties could be introduced by placing cards alongside one another. The respondent was then asked to rank the set of twenty standard occupations by ordering the blue cards. When he (or she) had assured the interviewer that he was satisfied with this ordering, he was asked to indicate his assessment of the social standing of titles in his set of representative occupations by interpolating the white cards into the array of blue cards. The interviewer then recorded on the schedule the final ranks of all 40 occupations, ignoring the distinction between blue and white cards. Occupations which had been tied were given the same rank. Ranks were assigned consecutively starting with 1 for the topmost card or cards and working down to the last card or cards.

When the grading task was completed, the interviewer collected basic 'face-sheet' information from respondents and also mentioned that in some cases we would like to interview respondents again about a fortnight after the first occasion. If the respondent agreed in principle to grant a second interview, possible dates and times were noted. Interviewers did not, however, know which respondents would in fact be interviewed again, and when repeat interviews were carried out they were always conducted by an interviewer other than the one who had performed the first interview. The second interview differed from the first only in that collection of some 'face-sheet' items was omitted. The occupations ranked were, of course, identical on the two occasions.

Response and non-response

In planning the national inquiry we were aware that a high response rate was not to be expected, partly because of the 'decay' in the electoral registers, but mainly because of the difficulty which interviewers would encounter in trying to persuade sample members to undertake a rather unusual card-sorting task. We relied, however, on empirical evidence which suggests that a low response rate is not likely to be a biasing factor in an occupation grading study. All previous studies of this kind have suggested that differences among persons in their assessment of occupations display virtually no social structuring, and our own more detailed investigations of this point (reported in Appendix A) led to the same

* We wish to acknowledge the most helpful collaboration of Mrs. Joan MacFarlane Smith, then Director of Field Services at BMRB, and of her colleagues.

negative conclusion. Thus differences in response rates between social collectivities whether of class, age or sex, are not likely to introduce distortions into the gradings. Furthermore, the data of the Oxford inquiry enable us to make an informed guess at the effect of non-response on gradings in that we were able to compare the data for our 160 respondents who performed the grading task on two occasions with the data for 42 respondents who performed it once and refused to repeat it on a second occasion. This guess rests, of course, on the supposition that the relevant characteristics of the once-interviewed lie somewhere between those of the twice-interviewed and those of the complete non-responders. The correlation between the over-all means (computed over all four dimensions and both occasions for 160 respondents, see Appendix A) of the twice-interviewed and those of the once-interviewed (computed over the same four dimensions for 42 respondents) is 0·989 for the forty occupations listed in Table A1.*

To achieve the required 620 interviews, 1,363 addresses were issued to interviewers[†] in the 60 polling districts selected by our sampling procedure, which is set out in detail in Appendix C. In computing the response rate we omit 64 of these attempted contacts because the quota of interviews for their polling districts had been completed before they were found (or, if found, before the date arranged for interviewing). Among the contacts, 180 were not interviewed because they lay outside the age limits of 20–64 years which define the population of potential respondents. Omitting these two categories gives us an achieved response of 620 out of a possible 1,119, which represents a rate of 55 per cent: 304 of the respondents were male and 316 female. The non-response consisted of 57 empty or no longer existent addresses, 259 non-contacts, 181 refusals of one sort or another, and 2 schedules rejected because of interviewer errors (these were of course reused). A more detailed analysis is given in Table C1.[‡]

However, it should also be observed that our sampling procedure included an application of Kish's (1965) selection tables to persons at a sampled address who were not on the electoral register for that address (including young persons whose eighteenth birthday was shown as falling within the life of the register). This was undertaken expressly to compensate for the effects of the decay of registers, and there are thus grounds for discounting in our calculation of response rate the 38 addresses which had been demolished or could not be found, the 19 which were empty, the 22 persons who were deceased, and the 169 persons who had moved from, or were not known at, the sampled address. Working on this alternative basis, we arrive at a response rate of 71 per cent.

---

* Analysis of the data for the once-interviewed showed that their gradings, when compared with those analysed in Table A2, contain a somewhat larger error component, a reduced common general factor, and an Occupations x Respondents term which is about twice as great.

† More were drawn but the surplus was held in reserve by fieldwork supervisors. Interviewers were initially issued with 50% more names than the number of interviews required because it was realized (a) that a substantial proportion of contacts would be outside the age-range defining the population and (b) that the decay of the electoral registers would result in a high rate of non-contact.

‡ What is not known is the proportion of non-responders who lay outside our age limits and who unduly inflate the non-response rate.

As earlier noted, one in eight of the 620 schedules was printed in duplicate by the computer in the hope that estimates of respondent inconsistency could be derived from about 10 per cent of respondents. In fact, 62 of the 77 respondents for whom a duplicate was printed were interviewed on a second occasion.

Checking and scoring procedures

The face-sheet information for each interview, and the ranks assigned to occupations, were recorded on punched cards. Since the interview schedules contained only the titles and not the reference numbers of the occupations graded, an automatic checking procedure was employed to ensure that each particular rank was matched to the correct reference number in the correct schedule, which had been recorded on magnetic tape as the schedules were drawn up and printed. This automatic check was supplemented by both systematic and random visual checks in which a listing of the complete data (reference numbers plus ranks) was compared directly with the schedules. In this way we were able to assure ourselves that no systematic errors had crept into the matching of ranks to occupation reference numbers and that the accuracy of the card-punching was very high indeed.

In the London pilot inquiry, which is reported in Appendix B, we had tried out a commensuration procedure which had proved to be highly satisfactory, and we adopted this without alteration in the main inquiry. The procedure involves using each respondent's centred and standardized gradings of the twenty standard occupations as a kind of yardstick against which his gradings of representative occupations can be measured. However, the image of a yardstick conveys an impression of greater precision than can in reality be attained when one set of gradings is scored in terms of another.* The scoring of representative occupations which had been tied with standard occupations is a fairly easy matter, but some simple, arbitrary rules had to be invented to deal with representative occupations which were not so tied.

In order to construct the yardstick itself, the ranking of the standard occupations was separated from the ranking of the representative occupations and the standard occupations were renumbered consecutively from 1 (for the highest ranked) exactly as they would have been numbered if ranks had been recorded before the representative titles were interpolated in the grading array. The renumbered ranks of the standard occupations were then treated as scores, and were centred about a mean of zero and standardized to a sum of squares of one. Signs of the centred and standardized scores were reflected so that high-grade occupations had positive scores and low-grade occupations had negative scores.

* It should be noted that, although one and the same set of twenty standard occupations was graded by each respondent before he was presented with his peculiar set of representative occupations, no attempt was made to allow for the fact that the correlations among gradings of standard occupations are far from perfect. Each respondent's representative occupations were scored in terms of his own ranking of the standard occupations. In fact the mean correlation between respondent's gradings of the standard occupations (computed by the analysis of variance methods of Appendix A) is 0·53 for the sample of 620. The comparable correlation for the 62 respondents who completed the task on two occasions is 0·58. Of the remaining 42% of the variance, 23% is due to respondent disagreement and 19% is error.

The application of the yardstick to the representative occupations involved the deployment of four rules. In the following statement of the rules the term 'level' is used to refer to a set of one or more *standard* titles which were assigned to a certain position by the respondent, and the term 'rank' is used to refer in an exactly analogous manner to a *representative* occupation or set of occupations lying at the same position in the grading distribution. It should be noted that, in these rules, a level or rank containing several tied occupations is given no more weight than a level or rank containing only a single occupation.

(1) A representative occupation which was tied with a level of the standard occupations was given the standardized score of that level.

(2) If k ranks of representative occupations lay between standard level a and standard level b, the difference between the standardized scores of a and b was divided by $k + 1$ to give an increment i. The representative rank adjacent to a was then assigned the score of a plus i, the next representative rank was assigned the score of a plus $2i$ and so on down to the representative rank nearest to b, to which was assigned the score of b minus i. In other words, the standardized difference between standard levels was split into equal intervals by the number of ranks of representative occupations lying between the two levels.

(3) In order to assign a score to representative ranks which were graded above the topmost standard level, a mean interval was calculated for the upper part of the distribution of standardized scores. This was computed by summing the intervals between all neighbouring levels of standard occupations which had a positive standardized score and dividing the sum by the number of intervals. An increment j was defined as one half of this mean interval. The representative rank immediately above the topmost standard level t was assigned the standardized score of t plus j. The representative rank next above this was given the score of t plus $2j$, and so on.

In the 620 schedules of the main inquiry (excluding those for second interviews) 207 representative titles were placed by respondents above their topmost standard titles.

(4) The procedure for assigning scores to representative ranks which were placed below the lowest standard level (of which there were 596) was the mirror image of rule (3).

5. SOME PROPERTIES OF THE SCALE

In the last section of the preceding chapter we described the scoring procedures which we applied to the empirical gradings of occupation titles obtained in the national inquiry. Before the scores thus produced were subjected to further analysis, one preliminary adjustment was made. The purpose of this was to set the mean score of the lowest-graded occupation to a value of 5 and the mean score of the highest-graded occupation to a value of 95. The adjustment* was effected by multiplying each score by the constant $m = 25 \cdot 9556$ and expressing the means to a base of 5. When this scaling procedure had been undertaken, the means of the 860 representative titles had a range from 5 to 95, a mean of $51 \cdot 25$ and a standard deviation of $63 \cdot 89$.

The scale values of the 124 categories were then computed by averaging scores over all occupation titles in a category and over all respondents grading those titles (but excluding the second gradings of the 10 per cent of respondents who completed the task on a second occasion). The values obtained are reported in Table 6.4; i.e. in the following chapter along with further information relevant to the actual application of our scale to occupational data. The main purpose of the present chapter is to report analyses which provide estimates of the relative importance of the several sources of variance in occupation gradings which were distinguished in Chapter 3 and thus give some indication of the reliability of the scale. We also consider the matter of certain apparent anomalies and imperfections in the scale.

Components of the variance of gradings

The first item of variance to be determined is the extent of *respondent inconsistency*. This is estimated from the gradings of the 62 respondents (10 per cent of the sample) who repeated the task on a second occasion.

If we look only at a single representative occupation † we may distinguish three sources of variance in the grading of that occupation: the disagreements among respondents when each respondent's scores for an occupation are averaged over the two occasions; the shift between occasions when the score for each occasion is averaged over all respondents grading the occupation; and the residual term representing differential shifts. In order to examine these effects, the scores

---

* The procedure involved (a) centring the scores about their overall mean; (b) multiplying each score by the constant $m = \dfrac{a_{\max} - a_{\min}}{95 - 5}$ where $a_{\max}$ is the mean score of the highest-graded occupation and $a_{\min}$ is the mean score of the lowest-graded occupation; and (c) adding $5 - ma_{\min}$ to each score.

† Looking at all occupations which were graded on two occasions we find an upward mean shift of $3 \cdot 08$ points between first and second occasion, accounting for a sum of squares of 5878. This occurs in spite of the fact that, for each occasion, the gradings of representative occupations were scored in terms of the gradings of standard occupations obtained on that occasion.

from both occasions for the 62 respondents were centred about their mean and multiplied by the constant m, and the sums of squares for the three terms were aggregated over all occupations for which estimates happened to be available: i.e. those which occurred on the repeat interview schedules.* Table 5.1 shows the results of this aggregation. Because several occupations were graded by only one respondent it is not possible in practice to distinguish between variance due to shifts and variance due to differential shifts. These two sources are therefore collapsed into a single Within-respondents term, which yields a variance of $s_i^2 = 180$ for respondent inconsistency.

The next source of variance to be investigated is that for *disagreements among respondents*. If we were to draw our estimate for this effect from the analysis of Table 5.1 we should arrive at a variance component of about 200. However, a more direct estimate may be obtained by reverting to analysis of the gradings by all 620 respondents. When our estimate of s_i^2 is substracted from the mean square for respondents grading the same occupation in Table 5.2 we obtain, as our estimate of respondent disagreement, $s_d^2 = 279$.

Both of these components are reported in Table 5.3, which also contains a statement of the model which underlies the analysis. All terms of the model except categories are assumed to be random. In order, finally, to estimate the extent of *heterogeneity among the occupations within a category*, it is necessary to specify a constant which represents a weighting for the variance component s_h^2. The constant employed is simply the average number of respondents grading a title, $\bar{n} \simeq 14$, and this yields a variance component for heterogeneity of $s_h^2 = 62$. A similar rough-and-ready approximation to the weighting constant for the category variance, $\bar{o} \simeq 7$, yields an estimate of $k^2 = 192$.

The percentages in the last column of Table 5.3 give us an idea of the relative importance of the various sources of error in the variance of a *single* grading. Although disagreement and inconsistency together account for almost two-thirds of this variance, it must be appreciated that no scale value is derived from a single grading, and that the proportionate importance of disagreement and inconsistency declines as more and more gradings are aggregated in the estimate of the position of an occupation or a category. It is possible to gain an impression of the degree of reliability of scale values (i.e. category means) which has been achieved so long as we are willing to make two assumptions: first, that every score is independent of every other score; and second, that the effect of employing $\bar{n}$ and $\bar{o}$ in Table 5.3 is a fair approximation to the estimates which would have been obtained if every occupation had been graded by exactly the same number of respondents and if every category had been represented by exactly the same number of occupations. (In addition we must suppose that our selections of representative occupations behave as if they were random samples.)

Several coefficients might be calculated, but only one will be presented here as an illustration of the degree to which disagreement and inconsistency shrink in significance when gradings are averaged. This coefficient is an estimate of the

---

* With the exception of one title which a respondent failed to grade on both occasions.

TABLE 5.1

Analysis of those occupations for which one or more repeated gradings were obtained in the main grading inquiry. The sums of squares have been summed over all such occupations.

Source	d.f.	Sum of squares	Mean square
Respondents	572	327940	573·32
Within respondents	1231	221302	179·77

TABLE 5.2

Analysis of gradings of 860 occupation titles by 620 respondents in the main grading inquiry. Each title belongs to one or other of 124 categories.

Source	d.f.	Sum of squares	Mean square
Categories of the scale	123	2516394	20458·49
Occupations within the same category	736	989749	1344·77
Respondents grading the same occupation	11499	5278836	459·07
Total	12358	8784980	710·87

TABLE 5.3

Expectations of mean squares and components of the variance of gradings of occupations in the main grading inquiry.

Source	Expectation	Mean square	Variance component	Variance component %
Categories	$s_i^2 + s_d^2 + \bar{n}s_h^2 + \bar{n}\,\bar{o}\,k^2$	20458·49	191·77	27
Heterogeneity within a category	$s_i^2 + s_d^2 + \bar{n}s_h^2$	1344·77	61·63	9
Respondent disagreement	$s_i^2 + s_d^2$	459·07	279·29	39
Respondent inconsistency	s_i^2	179·77	179·77	25
			712·47	100

correlation which would be observed if another investigator, using our categories, were to replicate our procedures for choosing a new set of representative occupatio and obtain gradings of them. The correlation is the correlation between our scale values for the 124 categories and those of the hypothetical replicator. The effect of averaging occupation means over approximately seven titles in each category is to deflate s_h^2 by a factor of 7, bringing it down from 62 to 9. The effect of averaging individual gradings over 100 responses in each category is to deflate $s_i^2 + s_d^2$ from 459 to 4·6. These deflated variances are clearly pretty small in comparison to the variance of the category mean, $k^2 = 192$. Thus the correlation between the two sets of category means would be of the order of,

$$\frac{k^2}{k^2 + \frac{1}{o} s_h^2 + \frac{1}{n\,o}(s_i^2 + s_d^2)} \simeq 0·93 \ .$$

Validity of scale values

Because the criterion of validity of our scale is internal to the method by which it was constructed, it is possible to estimate the scale's validity from the gradings, though it must be borne in mind that this coefficient refers, not to the validity of the scale as applied to a population of employed men, but simply to the diversity of occupational roles within categories. The coefficient appropriate to the former type of validity is that which would be obtained if men in a representative sample of the population were assigned to their positions on the scale, and their scale values were then compared with direct popular assessments of their particular occupations. The coefficient appropriate to the latter type of validity is the intracategory correlation among occupation titles,* and it may be expressed in terms of variance components as

$$\frac{k^2}{k^2 + s_h^2 + \frac{1}{n}(s_i^2 + s_d^2)} = 0·67 \ .$$

This coefficient is the analogue of the square of an ordinary validity coefficient that is, a correlation between a measuring instrument and an appropriate criterion It is customary, however, to purify a validity coefficient of errors due to unreliability in the criterion. The equivalent correction, applied to the validity ratio,

---

* If there were only two occupation titles, X and Y, in a category the coefficient would be more or less equal to an ordinary product-moment correlation between occupation X and occupation Y over all categories. The difficulty with this formulation is of course the difficulty of deciding which occupation shall be called X and which shall be called Y. This problem is formally identical to the problem which faced biometricians when they sought to calculate the correlation between characteristics of twins. The solution which they adopted was to write down each pair twice, once in the order A–B and then in the order B–A, and to compute the correlation between the resulting double-length columns of observations (Fisher, 1963, ch. VII). Equivalently, they employed analysis of variance to compute the intraclass (i.e. intrafamilial) correlation between twins. This is readily generalized to any number of sibs in a family, or occupations in a category, though strictly it requires that the numbers should be uniform.

consists in simply omitting the last term from the denominator. The rationale for this is that the contribution of respondent inconsistency and disagreement is a function of the number of respondents grading each occupation, and this could in principle be increased indefinitely, thus reducing the last term of the denominator to vanishing point. The square of the validity coefficient, after correction for attenuation due to the unreliability of the criterion, is then

$$\frac{k^2}{k^2 + s_h^2} = 0.76.$$

Until more direct evidence becomes available, the complement of this value, 0·24, is the best estimate we have of the proportion of error introduced by ascribing one and the same position on our scale to every occupation in a category. The square root of 0·76 may be employed in correcting for attenuation a correlation between the scale and any other measure. The correction factor appropriate to the correlation between two applications of the scale, is of course, 0·76. If, for example, in a study of occupational mobility, a correlation between fathers' and sons' positions on the scale is computed, then it may be divided by 0·76 to obtain an estimate of the underlying correlation between the true occupational positions.*

Differential error

The gradings for each category yield a Total sum of squares which represents the summed effects of both heterogeneity of occupation titles and disagreement and inconsistency among graders. This splits into two additive parts: the Between-titles sum of squares which reflects heterogeneity among titles, and the Within-titles sum of squares which represents disagreement or inconsistency among respondents grading particular titles. Each of these three sums of squares—that is, the Total and its two constituent parts—may be divided by its appropriate degrees of freedom to give a mean square, and the square root of the mean square may be taken as a standard deviation. In this way three standard deviations were computed for each category. In the following analysis the standard deviations were not weighted in spite of the fact that some of the Between-titles coefficients were derived from categories with only five titles while others were derived from categories with ten titles.

The average of the Total standard deviations is 22·5 and they have a standard deviation of 2·8, indicating that the scatter of gradings is very similar from category to category. The Within-titles standard deviations have a mean of 21·2 and a standard deviation of 2·8 which signifies little variation in extent of disagreement and inconsistency from category to category. They do however correlate 0·26

---

* Users of the scale who wish to correct the correlation between two applications of it should always pause to consider whether there might be some degree of contamination between determinations of occupational position. Such contamination might occur if constraints were operating to keep a man within a category when he changed his job. If such intra-category transition processes occur with more than chance frequency, then a correction employing the coefficient 0·76 will unduly inflate the estimate of underlying correlation.

with the scale values (the category means), indicating slightly more disagreement
or inconsistency over occupations in the higher categories. The regression of
standard deviation on mean is only 0·05, so that the difference between the
estimated standard deviation of the lowest category (which has a mean of 18)
and that of the highest category (which has a mean of 82) is about 3 scale points
as against an average standard deviation of 21 points.* (It may be noted that this
unweighted average is roughly equal to the square root of the mean square for
Respondent disagreement in Table 5.3.)

The mean of the Between-titles standard deviations is 35·4 (roughly equal to
the square root of the Heterogeneity mean square in Table 5.3), and its standard
deviation is 14·5, which indicates that we have not achieved a uniform scatter of
occupations within categories. On the other hand, the correlation between categor
means and Between-titles standard deviation is only −0·11, which suggests no
systematic tendency for scatter to increase as one moves along the scale. In their
relation with scale values, the Between- and Within-titles sources of variance tend
to cancel out, giving a correlation of 0·16 between the scale values and Total
standard deviations. The regression of Total standard deviation on scale value is
0·03, which implies a difference of 2 scale points between the scatter of the lowest
category and that of the highest category, compared with an average of 22·5. (In
fact the two estimates are 21·4 and 23·5.) This consideration, taken together with
the low value (2·8) of the standard deviation of the total standard deviations,
leads us to conclude that, in spite of differences among them in the extent of the
heterogeneity of their constituent occupations, the categories are remarkably
uniform in their overall standard deviations, and hence in the reliability of their
scale values. For all practical purposes the scale may be treated as having a constant standard error throughout its length. The Between-title and Total standard
deviations of each category are reported in Table 5.4.

Anomalies and imperfections

Some comparisons between occupation titles belonging to one category and
related titles belonging to another category suggest that anomalies, or apparent
anomalies, may occur when the scale is applied to the analysis of occupational
data, as in an occupational mobility study. These anomalies arise when an occupation title allied with a certain employment status has a scale value which equals
or exceeds the value assigned to the same title when it is in alliance with what
might be supposed to be a superior employment status. The following cases,
which represent all such that we have been able to detect, should serve to make
the nature and source of the difficulty clear.

---

* It is of course possible that some aspect of the grading or scoring procedure is responsible
for this slight but systematic effect.

TABLE 5.4

Between-title Standard deviation (representing heterogeneity of the standing of occupations) and Total standard deviation for each category

Category reference number	Number of titles	Between SD	Total SD
0101	5	33·29	22·83
0102	5	30·86	21·99
0103	5	31·52	26·27
0104	10	29·99	24·79
0201	10	39·32	26·95
0301	5	6·13	21·78
0302	10	30·14	25·34
0303	5	21·40	21·53
0304	10	22·90	21·69
0401	5	35·99	24·53
0402	5	29·65	22·04
0403	5	18·39	20·50
0404	5	13·28	24·85
0501	5	47·71	24·73
0601	5	35·90	23·85
0602	5	17·09	29·37
0603	5	28·65	20·29
0604	5	68·38	23·04
0605	5	30·01	24·37
0606	10	28·10	21·63
0607	10	33·69	19·36
0608	5	32·57	25·14
0609	10	30·13	24·38
0701	5	11·52	20·41
0801	5	38·91	24·29
0901	5	75·17	27·89
0902	5	44·54	22·84
0903	5	18·05	21·21
1001	10	52·22	26·90
1002	5	22·96	22·86
1101	10	24·64	22·66

Category reference number	Number of titles	Between SD	Total SD
1102	10	27·87	23·36
1103	10	26·39	23·20
1201	10	16·58	22·96
1202	5	50·19	22·91
1203	5	62·10	22·45
1301	5	31·96	25·88
1401	5	59·79	23·61
1402	5	60·81	22·80
1403	5	39·83	21·81
1404	10	31·21	20·73
1405	5	15·35	22·41
1406	10	41·56	26·76
1407	10	18·54	20·49
1501	5	25·33	23·77
1601	5	38·55	20·25
1701	10	27·05	17·84
1702	5	16·67	18·47
1703	10	20·32	19·87
1704	5	25·29	28·74
1801	10	31·21	21·03
1802	10	30·57	20·77
1803	5	51·22	27·29
1901	10	48·03	23·27
1902	5	44·87	26·52
1903	5	30·05	16·83
1904	10	34·80	23·01
1905	5	17·85	18·31
1906	5	35·75	21·20
2001	10	47·36	26·50
2101	10	38·04	25·78
2102	5	32·99	18·25

Category reference number	Number of titles	Between SD	Total SD
2201	5	15·21	20·49
2202	10	33·86	22·22
2203	5	62·90	26·36
2301	5	56·70	23·39
2302	5	33·74	20·46
2303	10	37·21	24·19
2304	10	60·28	23·64
2401	10	36·49	23·56
2402	10	54·50	23·94
2501	5	54·59	23·84
2601	5	17·45	19·50
2801	5	58·54	21·72
2901	10	27·38	17·97
3001	5	33·68	19·59
3002	10	22·65	20·26
3003	10	19·96	18·99
3004	10	19·16	17·66
3005	10	24·51	19·20
3006	10	42·72	24·75
3007	5	49·62	22·28
3008	5	69·18	22·19
3101	10	21·00	19·51
3102	5	69·14	23·34
3103	10	24·47	18·72
3104	5	48·54	20·99
3105	5	41·16	27·98
3106	10	32·99	21·92
3107	10	18·06	17·10
3108	5	49·99	21·51
3109	5	19·59	21·20
3110	5	24·31	20·51

Category reference number	Number of titles	Between SD	Total SD
3111	10	13·13	18·81
3112	5	24·29	17·19
3201	10	41·85	20·86
3202	10	33·60	19·22
3203	5	35·78	20·70
3204	10	37·62	21·49
3301	5	83·99	25·50
3302	10	20·31	17·30
3401	5	52·58	28·91
3402	5	23·16	22·23
3403	5	35·20	22·21
3501	10	39·18	29·49
3502	5	38·55	22·98
3601	5	41·58	26·41
3602	10	21·67	23·41
3603	5	49·91	20·10
3604	10	27·31	20·85
3605	5	38·26	21·89
3606	5	28·15	19·27
3701	5	31·64	22·52
3702	5	31·98	21·98
3703	5	51·61	19·96
3801	5	26·22	22·77
3901	10	37·99	24·47
4001	5	56·29	22·44
4002	5	38·94	23·16
4101	5	26·73	24·05
4201	10	36·01	20·87
4301	5	45·06	24·08
4401	5	37·14	22·08
4501	5	39·29	23·50
	860		

(1) Category 1002 covers men in only one unit group—218: draughtsmen, technical illustrators, various types of designer, etc.—who are working on their own account with less than 25 employees (employment status code 2), and has a scale value of 63. Category 0201 covers men in a number of unit groups, including 218, who are 'large' employers, that is, have 25 or more employees (employment status code 1), and it has a scale value of 61. Thus, a man running, say, his own technical drawing firm who expanded his labour force from under to over 25 would thereby slightly *diminish* his score on our scale. This anomaly comes about because category 1002 isolates what is in fact a relatively high-ranking group of occupations, whereas category 0201 merges this unit group with others which are generally lower in rank.

(2) A similar situation arises in the case of categories 1202 and 0404. The former is a 'small' employer category (code 2), the latter a 'large' employer category (code 1). All five of the unit groups covered by 1202 are also covered by 0404—i.e. 005, 135, 136, 137 and 153 which include, *inter alia*, gardeners, warehousemen, packers, guards, and security men. However, category 1202 has a scale value of 57 and category 0404 has a value of only 54. This is chiefly a consequence of the fact that 0404 also comprises two other unit groups—146: street vendors and hawkers, and 168: launderers and dry-cleaners—the representative titles from which were ranked generally lower than those from the five common unit groups. (The titles selected for both categories can be seen in Table 4.2.) Category 1202 also had one representative title—'owner of security firm (with less than 25 employees)'—which·was ranked extremely high, possibly because 'security' was sometimes understood as 'securities'.*

(3) One further anomaly of this same kind also appears to occur with categories 2102 and 2001: 2102 is a 'self-employed without employees' category (code 3) and 2001 a 'self-employed with employees' category (codes 1 and 2). Yet while they have twelve unit groups in common—chiefly comprising minor professional occupations such as chiropodists, physiotherapists, and teachers and instructors of various kinds—the former category has a scale value of 70 and the latter has a value of only 65. [†] Thus, it would happen that, say, a chiropodist who took on

---

* It might be added here that it should not be assumed that the number of employees will in *all* cases be a significant determinant of the 'social standing' of entrepreneurial occupations. For example, categories 0903 and 0103 take in only one, and the same, unit group—149: finance and insurance brokers and financial agents—the former associating it with 'small' employer status (code 2), and the latter with 'large' employer status (code 1). Both categories receive the same scale value of 72 (actually at two places of decimals 0903 comes out just higher than 0103 and so is ranked above 0103 in Table 6.4). It might, then, seem that one has here a further anomalous case. However, this may be doubted in the light of the fact that three of the five representative titles from each category are virtually identical—except, of course, for the number of employees stated—and there is no tendency for those from 0103 to be ranked higher than those from 0903. 'Stockbroker' was graded at 67 in category 0103 and at 72 in category 0903; 'insurance broker' at 73 and 75; and 'mortgage agent' at 70 and 63.

† Category 2102 also includes unit group 149, but this does not appear to be in any way a source of the anomaly.

an assistant would in consequence decline several points in his position on our scale. However, while such a case could certainly be regarded as an anomaly, it is also worth noting that the gradings of the representative occupations in these two categories do suggest that, in popular opinion, being an employer does not in itself add much, if anything, to the 'social standing' of a person in a professional occupation. Moreover, it may well be that the more typical occupations in category 2001 are essentially proprietorial ones—e.g. owner of a language or secretarial school or of a riding school or a dancing academy—which would in fact be generally ranked lower than straightforward professional occupations in which the employment of others is not involved.

(4) Like category 1002 referred to in (1) above, category 2302 also comprises the single unit group 218, in this case linked with the employment status of 'employee' (code 7), and again this isolation of draughtsmen etc. gives rise to a difficulty. Category 2302 has a scale value of 62 as against a value of 57 for category 2202 which is a 'supervisory' category (code 6) and includes unit group 218 along with three others which cover chiefly clerical occupations. Thus, a draughtsmen who is promoted to a supervisory grade would in fact move down-wards on our scale.

(5) A somewhat similar situation occurs in the case of categories 2301 and 2201. The former covers employees in unit groups 126, 128, and 152—mainly traffic controllers, telegraph and radio operators, and policemen—and has a scale value of 65. The latter is a supervisory category covering the same three unit groups—plus 127: telephone operators—with a scale value of 64. Again, then, it is evident that movement from employee to supervisory grade within certain unit groups is incapable of being reflected by our scale. On examination, the difficulty proves to arise chiefly from the fact that two representative titles in category 2301 tended to be given very high rankings indeed—i.e. 'flight controller at airport' and 'police officer (CID)'. This may perhaps be taken as indicating that the selection of titles for this category was somewhat unbalanced; but it may also serve as a reminder that even within the same occupational area it may not be the case that *all* supervisory grades are regarded as generally more desirable than *all* employee grades.

(6) This last point is perhaps even more relevant in regard to one other instance of a discrepancy between the scale values of an employee and a supervisory category 3104 which includes unit groups 025, 027, 028, 041, and 151—chiefly telephone installers and repairmen, electricians, motor mechanics and fire brigade men—has a value of 51, whereas 3003 which covers supervisors in these and a number of other unit groups, scores only 47. In part, this discrepancy arises because the supervisory grades of certain relatively low-ranking occupations not covered by 3104 are included in 3003. But it would also seem important to note here that in the literature of industrial and occupational sociology evidence is quite frequently to be found of rank-and-file manual workers in particular having

serious doubts about the desirability of promotion to supervisory level—on grounds of both relative economic returns and intrinsic rewards and deprivations (cf. NIIP, 1951 and 1957; Goldthorpe *et al.,* 1968). In other words, it should not be assumed that an occupational classification which automatically placed supervisory above employee grades would thereby always accurately reflect popular assessments of general desirability: it too could well produce anomalies in individual cases.*

(7) Finally, one evident discrepancy also occurs between two 'managerial' categories with employment status codes which differ according to size of establishment. Category 1601, which is made up of 'working' managers in small establishments (code 5), takes in twenty-three unit groups covering a wide range of skilled manual occupations and has a scale value of 48. Category 0801 similarly relates to working managers but in large establishments (code 4), and its constituent unit groups are three of the twenty-three of 1601—005, 136, and 168—which cover gardeners, warehousemen, storekeepers, launderers, and dry-cleaners. Its scale value, however, is only 46—thus creating the possibility that a manager in one of these three unit groups could move to a more responsible and better-paid post in a larger enterprise and yet decline in his position on our scale. This would of course be anomalous, but it should be noted that in general the gradings of representative titles from managerial categories that we obtained indicated that size of establishment was not an important consideration in the assessment of 'social standing', and indeed there is no very evident reason for supposing that it should be. (It must be borne in mind that the criterion of 25 employees or more does *not* refer to the number under the manager's own command or control.)

Reasons for not modifying the scale

The anomalies which have been described raise the question of whether or not modifications should be made to the scale in order to eliminate them. While this would not be difficult to do in some *ad hoc* fashion, it seemed to us that it would none the less be a mistaken step, for the following reasons.

First, the anomalies in question are few in number and arise for the most part in relation to scale categories in which only a very small proportion of the total employed population is to be found (cf. Table 6.4). More important, though, it must be recognized that these anomalies are in fact no more than relatively conspicuous instances of some wider extent of imperfection which inheres in our scale—as imperfection must, whether overtly or not, in any scale that falls short of the ideal of complete validity. These instances are revealed as 'anomalies' simply because error arising out of heterogeneity within our scale categories happened in these cases to result in certain occupations being assigned relative

* For example, that of the miner reluctantly taking up a deputy's job because he is becoming too old to continue with better-paid work at the coal face. For the relative undesirability of supervisory posts within the mining industry, see Goldthorpe (1960).

scale values which seem to run counter to common-sense notions of the implications for 'social standing' of size of enterprise or position in a formal hierarchy. Thus, to remove these evident errors would not have the effect of making the scale perfect: it would serve only to reduce its imperfection by some unknown, but probably very slight, amount.*

Secondly, to tinker with the scale in this way would mean contravening our principle of maintaining a clear distinction between the procedures involved in its *construction* and in its *evaluation*—and with undesirable consequences. To attempt to 'correct' the scale by reallocating certain occupations from one category to another might produce an impression of greater validity; but in fact any benefits gained by increasing the homogeneity of categories in this manner would be clearly outweighed (a) by the greater difficulties that would thus be incurred in making inferences from the occupation gradings which were obtained to the position on the scale of occupations which were not graded; and (b) by the greater degree of uncertainty which such 'adjustments' would impart to the reliability coefficients which the construction of the scale enables us to calculate and to their standard errors of estimate.[†]

The difficulty which some users may face in applying the scale as it stands is that of admitting that statistical error may sometimes imply demonstrable sociological mistakes. Clearly, it would be difficult to argue that a man who has moved up several rungs in a well-defined occupational hierarchy has actually declined in his 'social standing'; and even if such an argument were advanced, the empirical findings of a grading study such as we report in this volume would tend to give the lie to it.

None the less, the temptation to remove error simply where it happens to carry the cachet of manifest mistake should be resisted. Error which is not actually known with such palpable certainty to be wrong (because the sociologist does not have an independent means, such as the relative location of occupations within a bureaucratically defined hierarchy, by which to check it) nevertheless remains wrong, and the estimates of standard error which may be obtained do not make—nor should they make—any distinction between demonstrable and covert error. Error in a scale should of course be minimized, and this we sought to achieve by the construction procedures that we followed. But once a scale— that is, a set of rules for projecting individuals on to an axis—has been drawn up, the important problem which then faces the constructor is that of providing a good estimate of the degree of error so that error can be discounted in the use of the scale. Any attempt to further reduce error by changing the rules which constitute the scale must always to some unknown degree subvert the estimates of error which have been obtained.

* And, as suggested in the text above, the best that could be hoped for would be some *net* improvement—i.e. introducing some rule such as that all supervisory occupations should be graded above all rank-and-file occupations, would itself almost certainly entail some degree of error.

† Of course, if it were a case of producing an entirely new version of the scale, involving a further empirical grading enquiry, then a revision of the scale categories so as to eliminate errors evident in the present categorization would obviously be desirable, and no adverse consequence of this kind would arise.

6. USING THE SCALE

In this chapter, we present information and guidance which will be required by research workers who wish to apply our scale to occupational data. We begin with some observations on the collection and coding of such data which must be thoroughly understood by the research worker before he draws up his interview schedule or other research instrument. We then present tables for conversion of the basic data into elements of the scale. Finally we make a number of miscellaneous observations on the interpretation and nomenclature of the scale and we describe a possible collapse of the scale categories.

The recording of occupational data

The scale which we have developed is defined by a set of rules for assigning any employed male to a position on a certain conceptual axis: that of the general desirability of occupations as popularly assessed. If the scale is to be properly used, it must be possible to follow the rules which it comprises without curtailment or elaboration; and in this respect the quality of the occupational data to which the scale is to be applied is of crucial importance.

As the following section shows, use of the scale requires that occupations be coded according to OPCS procedures, which in turn requires that they should be identifiable in the OPCS index of occupation titles. This identification can be made with confidence only if occupations are described in a certain degree of detail. In most cases it will not be sufficient to have merely a two- or three-word description, since a description of this brevity will not enable a coder to decide with reasonable certainty (and in a way likely to be confirmed by other coders) which of two or more occupation titles in the index corresponds to the occupation he is trying to allocate. Uncertainty arising from incomplete occupation descriptions can be resolved only by the invention of *ad hoc* rules over and above those embodied in our scale. To the extent that such measures have to be adopted, then, strictly speaking, it is not in fact our scale, but some other set of rules, which is being employed, and one which cannot therefore be expected to give comparable results. If, for example, a man's occupation is described simply as 'assembler', it is impossible to identify it in the OPCS index, which distinguishes some 160 different kinds of assembler, distributed among 28 different unit groups. A rule to the effect that the occupation of 'assembler' when not further specified is to be coded to one of these groups would then obviously result in a much larger number of occupations being coded to that group, and rather fewer to each of the other 27 groups, than would occur if sufficiently detailed information had existed to allow our scale to be used without modification.

It must, therefore, be emphasized that research workers intending to use the scale should be at pains to ensure that the occupational information that they collect is of a quality which will permit OPCS coding procedures to be followed without undue difficulty. In the case of survey research, this requirement means that careful instructions must be given to interviewers (or included on postal questionnaires) on the way in which occupational data are to be recorded. It must be stressed that official occupational designations or 'everyday' names of occupations are not in themselves enough, and that what should be given wherever possible is a full description of the actual activities and operations in which the individual is involved in the day-to-day performance of his occupational role. For purposes of illustration, the following (edited) extracts are reproduced from the instructions given to interviewers working on the occupational mobility inquiry in connection with which our scale was initially developed.

OCCUPATION *
    In the space for Occupation you should record in full the informant's name for his job (for example, not just 'engineer' but 'chief electrical engineer' or 'consultant civil engineer') and a clear description of the kind of work he does and the nature of the operation performed.
    It is not possible to devise any one question that will fit all cases, and the interviewer should adapt her approach to suit the situation.
    If the informant's description of his occupation is too technical or vague, 'What kind of work is that?' or 'What do you actually do in that job?' are the most useful probes. The interviewer should realize that certain items that may present no difficulty to her because she is familiar with local industries may be incomprehensible to the staff at Nuffield College, and should therefore be explained. Sometimes informants will tell you in considerable detail what their job is 'concerned with' but not what they actually do. For example, your work is 'concerned with' market research, polls etc., but that does not tell us your occupation. There are some occupations which pose particular difficulties unless detailed information is collected. You should be on the look-out for such cases. Some examples are:
1. ENGINEER—It is not enough for somebody to answer 'engineer', as this can cover anything from a fully qualified professional to a semi-skilled operator. When an informant answers in vague terms, we in Nuffield would want to know what his full title is, and full details of the sort of work he is engaged in. For example, if he says 'electrical engineer', is he responsible for designing or planning the production or maintenance of electrical equipment, or, on the other hand, is he himself installing, maintaining, or repairing electrical equipment? In other words we want to know what the person himself actually does. This means that the term 'engineer' should never appear on its own unless an informant cannot answer about another person's occupation any more exactly than this.
2. MACHINIST—There are at least 1,000 different types of machinist, and the socio-economic grouping and/or social class depends on the type of machinist. There are 'machine grinders', 'machine cutters', 'machine casters', 'machine drillers', etc., and obviously we want to know which type of machinist the informant is.
3. MINERS—There are several types of miners. Some work at the coal face, underground, and some are suface workers, and the term 'miner' can include 'coal cutter', 'trimmers' (coal and coalmine), 'haulage hand', etc. We want always to know his full job description and whether or not he works at the coal face.

* These instructions are a modified and extended version of those used by the Social Survey Division of the OPCS. See Atkinson (1968, pp. 124–7).

4. COLLECTORS—This term covers nearly 80 different types of worker. For example, there are 'debt', 'rent', 'meter', 'rate'. and 'salvage' collectors, and 'collectors of customs and excise', to name a few.

5. TECHNICIANS—The term technician also has a wide range of usage and can be applied over almost the whole range of the social class and socio-economic groupings. Here we want to know whether the informant is, for example, a surgical technician or a radar technician, a cine technician or any of the other approximately 40 different types of technical workers. We also want to know exactly what he does. Sometimes people who describe themselves as technicians turn out to be electrical fitters or generating station attendants, and this is the kind of detail we want.

6. LABORATORY ASSISTANTS—Here again this occupation may be used to describe someone who merely washes the utensils and instruments and cleans the laboratory generally. Whenever this occupation is given, describe fully the duties of the informant and the work he actually does.

7. CIVIL SERVANTS—We want to know the informant's job within the Civil Service, i.e. what he actually does. However, you should always continue by giving the informant card I, and asking him in what category he would place his job. This card should also be used in those cases where Civil Servants refuse to specify the kind of work they do.
[The contents of card I were: Administrative; Executive; Clerical Officers; Clerical Assistants; Typists; Inspectorate; Messengers; Post Office; Professional Works Group; Technical Works Engineering and Allied Classes; Draughtsmen; Scientific Officer; Experimental Officer; Scientific Assistants (Technicians).]

8. REGULARS IN ARMED FORCES—Get rank and corps.

As you see, these general headings like 'Machinist' or 'Miner' etc. are not sufficient in themselves and the fullest description should be given when such occupations are mentioned by the informant. You should consider whether what you have elicited gives you and the coders a clear idea of how the informant spends a typical day, not minute by minute, but in terms of the skills he is using, both mental and physical. Never suggest the type of job to the informant, always ask him to describe it in his own words. REMEMBER: NO JOB IS SELF-EXPLANATORY.

In addition to a detailed description of individuals' occupational roles, the use of our scale also requires information on the employment status with which a given role is associated, so that one of the codes shown in Table 4.1 can be assigned. In the main, the details which need to be recorded are evident from the codes, but there are two points which call for special attention.

(1) In the case of men who 'have their own business', it is important to determine the precise nature of this—that is, whether it is a company, a partnership etc.—since, following OPCS procedures, this could affect whether an 'employer' or a 'manager' code should be given.

(2) In the case of men who are of employer or managerial status, it is important to ensure that the number of employees reported refers to the number employed *in the establishment in which the individual in question works* and not to the number under his own command or control or to the number employed in any firm or other organization of which that establishment may be a part. (The OPCS

definition of an 'establishment' is to be found in the *Standard Industrial Classification,* 1968, p. iii.)*

Finally, it should be specifically provided for that each occupational description is accompanied by information on the industry of the establishment in which the individual in question is employed—'industry' being here broadly understood as 'area of economic activity' so as to include such categories as 'education', 'local government', 'defence' etc. This information may often be of some general value in identifying occupations in the OPCS Index, since one way in which occupation titles are systematically qualified is by industry; and moreover in a certain number of cases industrial information is in fact essential for correct coding. For example, with labourers and other unskilled manual workers the industry of the establishment in which they are employed is the main criterion which governs their allocation among the unit groups, and this criterion may also enter into the coding of men of foreman status.

The coding of occupational data

As previously indicated, the use of our scale entails the coding of occupations by unit group and employment status following procedures established by the OPCS. These procedures, and the principles which underlie them, are fully set out in the *Classification of Occupations, 1970,* pp. xi—x and xiii—xvii, and there is therefore no need to restate them here. The three very minor modifications which the use of our scale calls for are the following.

(1) The OPCS allocate all members of armed forces, regardless of rank, to two unit groups: one (221) covering U.K. servicemen, the other (222), members of Commonwealth and foreign armed forces. We retain these groups but within each we distinguish three employment status levels: Officers (code 4); Non-Commissioned Officers (code 6); and Other Ranks (code 7).†

---

* It could well be argued that it would better serve the purposes of an occupational scale of the kind with which we are concerned if employers and managers *were* distinguished in terms of the number of employees under their direct or indirect supervision. Indeed, the OPCS itself recognizes that a classification of employers and managers by 'the degree of responsibility exercised' would in principle be preferable to the system it in fact adopts, but contends that it would be impracticable to obtain the required information in the Census (1970, p. xiii). The main consideration that influenced us in deciding to follow the OPCS was that of preserving as great a comparability as possible between Census data and those organized on the basis of our scale. However, it should be noted that no questions are included in the Census on the size of establishments which individuals own or in which they are employed, and we understand that coding decisions in these respects are taken on the basis of lists of establishments with 25 or more employees supplied by the Department of Employment. If an individual's establishment is not to be found in such a list, he is coded into the appropriate 'small' establishment category. For the purposes of this coding, an establishment is defined as any place of work whose employees' insurance cards are exchanged by their employer in a single bundle at the end of the insurance year. It is then possible that some discrepancy with Census data will arise where information on size of establishment is obtained directly from respondents (see below, p. 95).

† The six occupation grading units thus formed give rise to three of our scale categories by the amalgamation of the three pairs of units with the same employment status codes. See Table 6.4.

(2) We dispense with unit group 223–'Inadequately described occupations'–since such occupations cannot be given positions on our scale.

(3) The OPCS distinguish one unit group–072A: Rope, twine and net makers–which is exceptional in that it is restricted to workers in Northern Ireland. We retain this group but for convenience in computing give it the code number 224.

As may be appreciated from a reading of the pages of the *Classification of Occupations* cited above, the OPCS coding procedures are rather elaborate and not a few complexities and fine points arise.* It is therefore essential that coders should be thoroughly briefed and their work closely supervised until it is evident that they can follow the procedures correctly. In particular, attention should be given to the accuracy with which coders identify occupation titles in the index.

Where the quality of occupational data is high, the OPCS coding instructions, properly applied, should suffice in the majority of cases to make a reliable identification possible. However, there are cases, particularly where the quality of the data is poor, in which the coding instructions may be usefully supplemented by reference to the 'reversed' version of the OPCS index referred to in Chapter 4 (p. 27 above). This enables a coder to see at a glance the complete list of occupation titles comprised by a particular unit group, and the appropriate coding of a 'doubtful' occupation can often be determined by comparing the lists for the two or more unit groups to which it could conceivably be assigned. Indeed, whenever any degree of doubt arises about the coding of an occupation, it is desirable that the 'reversed' index should be consulted as a check.[†]

In treating the occupational data from the national occupational mobility inquiry in which we are engaged with our Oxford colleagues, we have for most occupational items on the interview schedule adopted a method of 'double' coding; that is, each occupational description was coded by two coders working independently and any disagreements were subsequently resolved by consultation between the coders who could, if they needed it, seek guidance from a coding supervisor. The agreed codings were then recorded and were checked by computer in order to identify any illegal codes, including impermissible combinations of occupation unit group codes with either employment status or industry codes. Where such illegal codes were revealed, a revised coding was made by a coding supervisor.

---

* The only inconsistency that we have noted arises over the employment status of men described as 'assistant foreman', 'assistant supervisor', etc. On p. xv it is indicated that these terms may be treated as equivalent to 'foreman' for coding purposes; but on p. xvii it is stated that the 'foreman' code is given to all persons returned as foreman or with one of the synonyms listed on p. xv but *excluding* 'assistant foreman', 'assistant supervisor', etc. Our recommendation would be that such titles *should* be taken as indicating supervisory status (i.e. code 6 should be used) on the grounds that the functions of men so described are in most cases likely to be closer to those of supervisors than to those of rank-and-file employees.

† Copies of this reversed index have been deposited with the Social Science Research Council's Survey Archive and may be obtained on application to The Director, Social Science Research Council Survey Archive, University of Essex, Wivenhoe Park, Colchester, Essex, CO4 3SQ.

In order to examine the reliability of this method of coding, the responses of some 300 respondents to six occupation questions were coded a second time, following the above procedures, and correlations were calculated between the scale values derived from the two sets of codes. These correlations ranged from 0·862 (for respondent's first job) to 0·938 (for his present job). The relatively low reliability for first job probably stems more from difficulty in ascertaining which of several early occupations should be taken as first job (following a rule formulated to exclude holiday jobs, pre-university and pre-apprenticeship 'filling-in' jobs, etc), than from difficulty in executing the procedures outlined above. Apart from this, the lowest reliability was 0·906, and this pertained to the occupation of the head of respondent's household when the respondent was aged 14.

Tables of the scale

Having recorded the unit group of an occupation (following the procedures of the *Classification of Occupations, 1970*) and its employment status (coded as in Table 4.1) the user of the scale must enter Table 6.1 to determine the category to which the occupation belongs and the scale value of that category. It is strongly recommended that the research worker should record all four of these items of information in his data matrix, (i.e. unit group, employment status, category, and scale value) and not only the last, since this will enable him, and other workers, to disaggregate the scale values and their associated categories into their constituent occupation grading units (combinations of unit group and employment status), which may then be reassembled for purposes which might not have been evident when the data were first recorded. Table 6.2 is provided as a convenient means of converting from category reference number to scale value or rank.

Tables 6.1 and 6.2 are laid out in forms which will be most convenient for the research worker who is transforming his coded data by personal inspection. For purposes of computer transformation, however, it is convenient to employ reference numbers which are consecutive rather than arbitrary, since sequential numbers can function as indices or subscripts of vectors. The arbitrary category reference numbers of Table 6.1 may therefore be replaced by the corresponding sequential reference numbers listed in Table 6.3. These sequential numbers have been assigned to the 124 categories in order of their projections on the scale. Table 6.3 is similar in format to Table 6.1 but with the sequential numbers in place of the arbitrary reference numbers. If a computer is employed to convert unit group and employment status codes into category numbers and scale values, Table 6.3 may be introduced as a look-up table, in which '125' signifies 'missing codes' or 'impermissible occupation grading unit'. In order to convert from sequential category number to scale value, a look-up vector of 125 scale values must then be entered, the first 124 being the scale values in the order in which they appear in Table 6.4, and the final value being a code which signifies 'not applicable' or 'value missing'. (*continued on p. 95*)

TABLE 6.1

For converting from unit group (rows) and employment status (columns) to category reference number. A blank signifies an impermissible combination of unit group and employment status. Each cell of the table is an occupation grading unit and the entry in a cell is the reference number of a category followed by its scale value in parentheses.

Unit Group	Self-employed 25 or more employees 1	Self-employed less than 25 employees 2	Self-employed No employees 3	Manager 25 or more employees 4	Manager less than 25 employees 5	Foreman/Supervisor 6	Employee 7
001	3901 (58·15)	1201 (52·89)	3701 (43·98)		1601 (48·51)	3007 (48·34)	3203 (32·67)
002	3901 (58·15)	3901 (58·15)	4001 (37·18)	3901 (58·15)	3901 (58·15)	4101 (40·92)	4201 (31·49)
003	3901 (58·15)	3901 (58·15)	4002 (30·01)	3901 (58·15)	3901 (58·15)	4101 (40·92)	4201 (31·49)
004	3901 (58·15)	3901 (58·15)	4002 (30·01)	3901 (58·15)	3901 (58·15)	3006 (42·08)	3204 (28·35)
005	0404 (53·92)	1202 (57·24)	3703 (17·52)	0801 (45·58)	1601 (48·51)	4101 (40·92)	4201 (31·49)
006	3901 (58·15)	3901 (58·15)	4002 (30·01)	3901 (58·15)	3901 (58·15)	3007 (48·34)	3109 (35·53)
007	0303 (66·45)	1101 (53·85)	3603 (43·25)		1407 (54·99)	3007 (48·34)	3203 (32·67)
008	0402 (61·68)	1201 (52·89)	3701 (43·98)		1601 (48·51)	3007 (48·34)	3109 (35·53)
009	0303 (66·45)	1101 (53·85)	3603 (43·25)		1407 (54·99)	3007 (48·34)	3203 (32·67)
010	0402 (61·68)	1201 (52·89)	3701 (43·98)		1601 (48·51)	3004 (46·51)	3201 (35·55)
011							
012	0401 (55·53)	1201 (52·89)	3702 (41·43)		1601 (48·51)	3005 (43·72)	3201 (35·55)
013	0304 (63·29)	1103 (54·59)	3604 (41·18)		1407 (54·99)	3005 (43·72)	3107 (37·60)
014	0304 (63·29)	1103 (54·59)	3604 (41·18)		1407 (54·99)	3004 (46·51)	3107 (37·60)
015	0304 (63·29)	1103 (54·59)	3604 (41·18)		1407 (54·99)	3004 (46·51)	3111 (32·61)
016	0304 (63·29)	1103 (54·59)	3604 (41·18)		1407 (54·99)	3004 (46·51)	3107 (37·60)
017	0401 (55·53)	1201 (52·89)	3702 (41·43)		1601 (48·51)	3004 (46·51)	3201 (35·55)
018	0304 (63·29)	1103 (54·59)	3604 (41·18)		1407 (54·99)	3004 (46·51)	3111 (32·61)
019	0304 (63·29)	1103 (54·59)	3604 (41·18)		1407 (54·99)	3005 (43·72)	3107 (37·60)
020	0304 (63·29)	1103 (54·59)	3604 (41·18)		1407 (54·99)	3004 (46·51)	3111 (32·61)

Unit Group	Self-employed 25 or more employees 1	Self-employed less than 25 employees 2	Self-employed No employees 3	Manager 25 or more employees 4	Manager less than 25 employees 5	Foreman Supervisor 6	Employee 7
021	0304 (63·29)	1103 (54·59)	3604 (41·18)		1407 (54·99)	3004 (46·51)	3111 (32·61)
022	0401 (55·53)	1201 (52·89)	3702 (41·43)		1601 (48·51)	3004 (46·51)	3201 (35·55)
023	0401 (55·53)	1201 (52·89)	3702 (41·43)			3005 (43·72)	3201 (35·55)
024	0301 (64·04)	1102 (54·59)	3602 (42·70)		1407 (54·99)	3003 (47·49)	3102 (54·12)
025	0301 (64·04)	1102 (54·59)	3605 (35·24)		1407 (54·99)	3003 (47·49)	3104 (50·90)
026			3605 (35·24)			3003 (47·49)	3108 (35·67)
027	0301 (64·04)	1102 (54·59)	3602 (42·70)		1407 (54·99)	3003 (47·49)	3104 (50·90)
028	0301 (64·04)	1102 (54·59)	3602 (42·70)		1407 (54·99)	3003 (47·49)	3104 (50·90)
029	0401 (55·53)	1201 (52·89)	3702 (41·43)			3004 (46·51)	3201 (35·55)
030	0301 (64·04)	1102 (54·59)	3602 (42·70)				3102 (54·12)
031							
032						3004 (46·51)	
033	0304 (63·29)	1103 (54·59)	3604 (41·18)		1407 (54·99)	3004 (46·51)	3107 (37·60)
034	0302 (60·12)	1101 (53·85)	3603 (43·25)		1407 (54·99)	3008 (46·80)	3107 (37·60)
035	0304 (63·29)	1103 (54·59)	3604 (41·18)		1407 (54·99)	3004 (46·51)	3110 (35·03)
036	0304 (63·29)	1103 (54·59)	3604 (41·18)		1407 (54·99)	3004 (46·51)	3107 (37·60)
037	0304 (63·29)	1103 (54·59)	3604 (41·18)		1407 (54·99)	3002 (48·91)	3106 (45·57)
038	0304 (63·29)	1103 (54·59)	3604 (41·18)		1407 (54·99)	3002 (48·91)	3106 (45·57)
039	0401 (55·53)	1201 (52·89)	3702 (41·43)			3004 (46·51)	3107 (37·60)
040	0304 (63·29)	1103 (54·59)	3604 (41·18)		1407 (54·99)	3002 (48·91)	3201 (35·55)
041	0301 (64·04)	1102 (54·59)	3602 (42·70)		1407 (54·99)	3003 (47·49)	3104 (50·90)
042	0304 (63·29)	1103 (54·59)	3604 (41·18)		1407 (54·99)	3002 (48·91)	3106 (45·57)
043	0304 (63·29)	1103 (54·59)	3604 (41·18)		1407 (54·99)	3002 (48·91)	3106 (45·57)
044	0304 (63·29)	1103 (54·59)	3604 (41·18)		1407 (54·99)	3004 (46·51)	3111 (32·61)

045	0302 (60·12)	1101 (53·85)	3603 (43·25)	1407 (54·99)	3003 (47·49)	3103 (37·62)
046	0302 (60·12)	1101 (53·85)	3603 (43·25)	1407 (54·99)	3003 (47·49)	3103 (37·62)
047	0401 (55·53)	1201 (52·89)	3702 (41·43)	1601 (48·51)	3004 (46·51)	3201 (35·55)
048	0304 (63·29)	1103 (54·59)	3606 (33·89)	1407 (54·99)	3005 (43·72)	3111 (32·61)
049	0304 (63·29)	1103 (54·59)	3602 (42·70)	1407 (54·99)	3001 (48·55)	3101 (39·87)
050	0304 (63·29)	1103 (54·59)	3602 (42·70)	1407 (54·99)	3001 (48·55)	3101 (39·87)
051	0304 (63·29)	1103 (54·59)	3602 (42·70)	1407 (54·99)	3001 (48·55)	3101 (39·87)
052	0304 (63·29)	1103 (54·59)	3604 (41·18)	1407 (54·99)	3004 (46·51)	3106 (45·57)
053			3702 (41·43)		3002 (48·91)	3201 (35·55)
054	0401 (55·53)	1201 (52·89)	3702 (41·43)	1601 (48·51)	3004 (46·51)	3201 (35·55)
055	0302 (60·12)	1101 (53·85)	3603 (43·25)	1407 (54·99)	3002 (48·91)	3103 (37·62)
056	0304 (63·29)	1103 (54·59)	3602 (42·70)	1407 (54·99)	3001 (48·55)	3101 (39·87)
057	0304 (63·29)	1103 (54·59)	3606 (33·89)	1407 (54·99)	3004 (46·51)	3111 (32·61)
058	0304 (63·29)	1103 (54·59)	3604 (41·18)	1407 (54·99)	3002 (48·91)	3106 (45·57)
059	0304 (63·29)	1103 (54·59)	3604 (41·18)	1407 (54·99)	3004 (46·51)	3111 (32·61)
060	0304 (63·29)	1103 (54·59)	3606 (33·89)	1407 (54·99)	3005 (43·72)	3111 (32·61)
061	0304 (63·29)	1103 (54·59)	3604 (41·18)	1407 (54·99)	3004 (46·51)	3106 (45·57)
062	0304 (63·29)	1103 (54·59)	3604 (41·18)	1407 (54·99)	3005 (43·72)	3111 (32·61)
063	0304 (63·29)	1103 (54·59)	3604 (41·18)	1407 (54·99)	3005 (43·72)	3111 (32·61)
064	0401 (55·53)	1201 (52·89)	3702 (41·43)	1601 (48·51)	3005 (43·72)	3201 (35·55)
065	0401 (55·53)	1201 (52·89)	3702 (41·43)	1601 (48·51)	3005 (43·72)	3201 (35·55)
066	0401 (55·53)	1201 (52·89)	3702 (41·43)	1601 (48·51)	3005 (43·72)	3201 (35·55)
067	0304 (63·29)	1103 (54·59)	3606 (33·89)	1407 (54·99)	3005 (43·72)	3111 (32·61)
068	0304 (63·29)	1103 (54·59)	3606 (33·89)	1407 (54·99)	3005 (43·72)	3111 (32·61)
069	0304 (63·29)	1103 (54·59)	3604 (41·18)	1407 (54·99)	3005 (43·72)	3111 (32·61)
070	0304 (63·29)	1103 (54·59)	3606 (33·89)	1407 (54·99)	3005 (43·72)	3111 (32·61)
071	0304 (63·29)	1103 (54·59)	3606 (33·89)	1407 (54·99)	3005 (43·72)	3111 (32·61)

Unit Group	Self-employed 25 or more employees 1	Self-employed less than 25 employees 2	Self-employed No employees 3	Manager 25 or more employees 4	Manager less than 25 employees 5	Foreman/ Supervisor 6	Employee 7
072	0304 (63·29)	1103 (54·59)	3604 (41·18)		1407 (54·99)	3005 (43·72)	3111 (32·61)
073	0401 (55·53)	1201 (52·89)	3702 (41·43)		1407 (54·99)	3005 (43·72)	3201 (35·55)
074	0304 (63·29)	1103 (54·59)	3604 (41·18)		1407 (54·99)	3005 (43·72)	3111 (32·61)
075	0304 (63·29)	1103 (54·59)	3604 (41·18)		1407 (54·99)	3004 (46·51)	3106 (45·57)
076	0401 (55·53)	1201 (52·89)	3702 (41·43)			3005 (43·72)	3201 (35·55)
077	0304 (63·29)	1103 (54·59)	3604 (41·18)		1407 (54·99)	3005 (43·72)	3111 (32·61)
078	0304 (63·29)	1103 (54·59)	3604 (41·18)		1407 (54·99)	3005 (43·72)	3111 (32·61)
079	0304 (63·29)	1103 (54·59)	3604 (41·18)		1407 (54·99)	3005 (43·72)	3111 (32·61)
080	0304 (63·29)	1103 (54·59)	3604 (41·18)		1407 (54·99)	3005 (43·72)	3111 (32·61)
081	0401 (55·53)	1201 (52·89)	3702 (41·43)		1601 (48·51)	3005 (43·72)	3201 (35·55)
082	0401 (55·53)	1201 (52·89)	3702 (41·43)		1601 (48·51)	3005 (43·72)	3201 (35·55)
083	0304 (63·29)	1103 (54·59)	3606 (33·89)		1407 (54·99)	3005 (43·72)	3111 (32·61)
084	0304 (63·29)	1103 (54·59)	3606 (33·89)		1407 (54·99)	3005 (43·72)	3111 (32·61)
085	0304 (63·29)	1103 (54·59)	3604 (41·18)		1407 (54·99)	3005 (43·72)	3101 (39·87)
086	0304 (63·29)	1103 (54·59)	3604 (41·18)			3001 (48·55)	3107 (37·60)
087	0304 (63·29)	1103 (54·59)	3604 (41·18)		1407 (54·99)	3001 (48·55)	3101 (39·87)
088	0304 (63·29)	1103 (54·59)	3604 (41·18)		1407 (54·99)	3001 (48·55)	3111 (32·61)
089	0304 (63·29)	1103 (54·59)	3606 (33·89)		1407 (54·99)	3005 (43·72)	3111 (32·61)
090	0401 (55·53)	1201 (52·89)	3702 (41·43)		1601 (48·51)	3005 (43·72)	3201 (35·55)
091	0304 (63·29)	1103 (54·59)	3604 (41·18)		1407 (54·99)	3002 (48·91)	3106 (45·57)
092	0401 (55·53)	1201 (52·89)	3702 (41·43)		1601 (48·51)	3005 (43·72)	3201 (35·55)
093	0302 (60·12)	1101 (53·85)	3603 (43·25)		1407 (54·99)	3008 (46·80)	3103 (37·62)
094	0302 (60·12)	1101 (53·85)	3603 (43·25)		1407 (54·99)	3008 (46·80)	3103 (37·62)
095	0302 (60·12)	1101 (53·85)	3603 (43·25)		1407 (54·99)	3008 (46·80)	3103 (37·62)

096	0302 (60·12)	1101 (53·85)	3603 (43·25)		1407 (54·99)	3008 (46·80)	3103 (37·62)
097	0403 (62·83)	1201 (52·89)	3701 (43·98)		1601 (48·51)	3008 (46·80)	3202 (30·00)
098	0401 (55·53)	1201 (52·89)	3701 (43·98)		1601 (48·51)	3005 (43·72)	3202 (30·00)
099	0302 (60·12)	1201 (52·89)	3702 (41·43)		1601 (48·51)	3008 (46·80)	3201 (35·55)
100	0304 (63·29)	1101 (53·85)	3603 (43·25)		1407 (54·99)	3004 (46·51)	3103 (37·62)
101		1103 (54·59)	3606 (33·89)		1407 (54·99)	3005 (43·72)	3111 (32·61)
102						3004 (46·51)	3201 (35·55)
103							3110 (35·03)
104	0302 (60·12)	1101 (53·85)	3603 (43·25)		1407 (54·99)	3008 (46·80)	3110 (35·03)
105						3004 (46·51)	3111 (32·61)
106						3006 (42·08)	3204 (28·35)
107						3005 (43·72)	3302 (18·36)
108						3005 (43·72)	3302 (18·36)
109						3005 (43·72)	3302 (18·36)
110						3005 (43·72)	3302 (18·36)
111						3005 (43·72)	3302 (18·36)
112						3005 (43·72)	3302 (18·36)
113		1301 (40·93)	3801 (30·05)			3008 (46·80)	3302 (18·36)
114		1301 (40·93)	3801 (30·05)			3005 (43·72)	3302 (18·36)
115	0101 (66·24)		3401 (54·28)	0604 (65·85)		3006 (42·08)	3204 (28·35)
116	0401 (55·53)	1201 (52·89)	3703 (17·52)				1906 (76·71)
117	0101 (66·24)		3401 (54·28)	0603 (69·14)			3108 (35·67)
118							3112 (27·23)
119						3006 (42·08)	3112 (27·23)
120	0301 (64·04)	1102 (54·59)	3605 (35·24)		1407 (54·99)		3112 (27·23)
121	0301 (64·04)	1102 (54·59)	3605 (35·24)		1407 (54·99)		3112 (27·23)
122	0301 (64·04)	1102 (54·59)	3605 (35·24)		1407 (54·99)	3006 (42·08)	3112 (27·23)

80

Unit Group	Self-employed 25 or more employees 1	Self-employed less than 25 employees 2	Self-employed No employees 3	Manager 25 or more employees 4	Manager less than 25 employees 5	Foreman/ Supervisor 6	Employee 7
123	0104 (63·75)	0902 (56·50)		0604 (65·85)	1407 (54·99)	1905 (37·14)	3108 (35·67)
124					1407 (54·99)	3006 (42·08)	3108 (35·67)
125					1407 (54·99)	3006 (42·08)	2301 (64·84)
126				0604 (65·85)		2201 (64·30)	2401 (27·10)
127						2201 (64·30)	2301 (64·84)
128				0604 (65·85)		2201 (64·30)	3204 (28·35)
129						3006 (42·08)	3302 (18·36)
130			3801 (30·05)			3006 (42·08)	3204 (28·35)
131			3703 (17·52)				3302 (18·36)
132							3301 (28·33)
133	0501 (52·35)	1301 (40·93)	3801 (30·05)			3006 (42·08)	3302 (18·36)
134						3003 (47·49)	
135	0404 (53·92)	1202 (57·24)	3703 (17·52)	0801 (45·58)	1601 (48·51)	3006 (42·08)	3204 (28·35)
136	0404 (53·92)	1202 (57·24)	3703 (17·52)		1601 (48·51)	3006 (42·08)	3204 (28·35)
137	0404 (53·92)	1202 (57·24)	3703 (17·52)			3006 (42·08)	3204 (28·35)
138				0607 (68·98)	1406 (52·80)		
139	0201 (60·57)	1001 (56·02)	3502 (56·06)			2202 (56·95)	2303 (39·85)
140	0201 (60·57)	1001 (56·02)	3502 (56·06)			2202 (56·95)	2304 (34·62)
141	0201 (60·57)	1001 (56·02)	3502 (56·06)			2202 (56·95)	2304 (34·62)
142						1904 (61·14)	
143	0104 (63·75)	0902 (56·50)	3403 (38·96)	0605 (68·66)	1406 (52·80)	2203 (48·15)	2304 (34·62)
144						3006 (42·08)	3204 (28·35)
145							2401 (27·10)
146	0404 (53·92)	1203 (41·25)	3703 (17·52)		1501 (47·61)	2203 (48·15)	

147	0104 (63·75)	0902 (56·50)	3402 (46·62)			2203 (48·15)	2303 (39·85)
148	0201 (60·57)	1001 (56·02)	3502 (56·06)		1406 (52·80)	2203 (48·15)	2303 (39·85)
149	0103 (71·72)	0903 (71·74)	2102 (69·56)	0603 (69·14)	1406 (52·80)	3003 (47·49)	3104 (50·90)
150	0201 (60·57)	1001 (56·02)	3501 (30·78)	0605 (68·66)	1406 (52·80)	2201 (64·30)	2301 (64·84)
151				0609 (67·62)		2203 (48·15)	2401 (27·10)
152				0609 (67·62)			
153	0404 (53·92)	1202 (57·24)	3703 (17·52)	0701 (67·24)	1501 (47·61)	2601 (36·05)	2901 (22·95)
154	0101 (66·24)	0902 (56·50)	3402 (46·62)	0608 (59·23)	1405 (43·40)		
155			3703 (17·52)				
156	0101 (66·24)	0902 (56·50)	3403 (38·96)	0608 (59·23)	1403 (55·20)	2601 (36·05)	2501 (47·32)
157				0608 (59·23)	1405 (43·40)		2701 (——)
158							
159	0201 (60·57)	1001 (56·02)	3501 (30·78)	0608 (59·23)	1403 (55·20)	2601 (36·05)	2901 (22·95)
160			3703 (17·52)			2601 (36·05)	2901 (22·95)
161							2801 (37·44)
162	0301 (64·04)	1102 (54·59)	3605 (35·24)	0608 (59·23)	1405 (43·40)	2801 (37·44)	3302 (18·36)
163						3006 (42·08)	2901 (22·95)
164			3703 (17·52)			2601 (36·05)	2401 (27·10)
165						2203 (48·15)	3302 (18·36)
166	0501 (52·35)	1301 (40·93)	3801 (30·05)	0608 (59·23)	1601 (48·51)	3006 (42·08)	2801 (37·44)
167	0301 (64·04)	1102 (54·59)	3602 (42·70)	0608 (59·23)	1405 (43·40)	2801 (37·44)	
168	0404 (53·92)	1203 (41·25)	3703 (17·52)	0801 (45·58)	1601 (48·51)	3006 (42·08)	3204 (28·35)
169	0301 (64·04)	1102 (54·59)	3601 (45·94)	0608 (59·23)	1405 (43·40)		3105 (50·35)
170						3006 (42·08)	3204 (28·35)
171	0201 (60·57)	1001 (56·02)	3501 (30·78)	0608 (59·23)	1405 (43·40)		
172						2203 (48·15)	2402 (32·42)
173				0601 (79·53)			

Unit Group	Self-employed 25 or more employees 1	Self-employed less than 25 employees 2	Self-employed No employees 3	Manager 25 or more employees 4	Manager less than 25 employees 5	Foreman/ Supervisor 6	Employee 7
174				0603 (69·14)	1404 (62·19)		
175				0606 (66·11)	1404 (62·19)		
176				0606 (66·11)	1404 (62·19)		
177				0606 (66·11)	1404 (62·19)		
178				0606 (66·11)	1404 (62·19)		
179				0605 (68·66)	1406 (52·80)		
180				0607 (68·98)	1404 (62·19)		
181	1701 (82·05)	1701 (82·05)	1701 (82·05)				1801 (76·29)
182	1702 (74·94)	1702 (74·94)	1702 (74·94)				1801 (76·29)
183	2001 (65·25)	2001 (65·25)	2102 (69·56)	0609 (67·62)	1402 (65·68)	1904 (61·14)	1904 (61·14)
184	1703 (73·06)	1703 (73·06)	1703 (73·06)				1802 (70·92)
185	2001 (65·25)	2001 (65·25)	2102 (69·56)	0609 (67·62)	1402 (65·68)	1904 (61·14)	1904 (61·14)
186	1703 (73·06)	1703 (73·06)	1703 (73·06)				1801 (76·29)
187	2001 (65·25)	2001 (65·25)	2102 (69·56)	0609 (67·62)	1402 (65·68)	1904 (61·14)	1904 (61·14)
188	2001 (65·25)	2001 (65·25)	2102 (69·56)	0609 (67·62)	1402 (65·68)	1904 (61·14)	1904 (61·14)
189	2001 (65·25)	2001 (65·25)	2102 (69·56)	0609 (67·62)	1402 (65·68)	1904 (61·14)	1904 (61·14)
190						1904 (61·14)	1904 (61·14)
191	2001 (65·25)	2001 (65·25)	2102 (69·56)	0609 (67·62)	1402 (65·68)	1904 (61·14)	1904 (61·14)
192							1801 (76·29)
193	2001 (65·25)	2001 (65·25)	2102 (69·56)	0609 (67·62)	1402 (65·68)		1904 (61·14)
194	2001 (65·25)	2001 (65·25)	2102 (69·56)	0609 (67·62)	1402 (65·68)		1904 (61·14)
195	1703 (73·06)	1703 (73·06)	1703 (73·06)				1802 (70·92)
196	1703 (73·06)	1703 (73·06)	1703 (73·06)				1802 (70·92)
197	1703 (73·06)	1703 (73·06)	1703 (73·06)				1802 (70·92)

198	1703 (73·06)	1703 (73·06)	1703 (73·06)	0606 (66·11)	1404 (62·19)		1802 (70·92)
199	2001 (65·25)	2001 (65·25)	2102 (69·56)			1903 (64·05)	1903 (64·05)
200	1703 (73·06)	1703 (73·06)	1703 (73·06)				1802 (70·92)
201	1703 (73·06)	1703 (73·06)	1703 (73·06)				1802 (70·92)
202	1703 (73·06)	1703 (73·06)	1703 (73·06)				1802 (70·92)
203	1703 (73·06)	1703 (73·06)	1703 (73·06)				1802 (70·92)
204	1703 (73·06)	1703 (73·06)	1703 (73·06)				1802 (70·92)
205	1703 (73·06)	1703 (73·06)	1703 (73·06)				1802 (70·92)
206	0102 (66·86)	0901 (53·87)	2101 (60·89)	0602 (72·19)	1401 (57·81)		1901 (59·38)
207	0102 (66·86)	0901 (53·87)	2101 (60·89)	0602 (72·19)	1401 (57·81)		1901 (59·38)
208	0102 (66·86)	0901 (53·87)	2101 (60·89)	0602 (72·19)	1401 (57·81)	1901 (59·38)	1901 (59·38)
209	1701 (82·05)	1701 (82·05)	1701 (82·05)				1801 (76·29)
210	1701 (82·05)	1701 (82·05)	1701 (82·05)				1801 (76·29)
211	1703 (73·06)	1703 (73·06)	1703 (73·06)				1801 (76·29)
212	1702 (74·94)	1702 (74·94)	1702 (74·94)				1802 (70·92)
213	1704 (62·33)	1704 (62·33)	1704 (62·33)				1803 (63·88)
214	1701 (82·05)	1701 (82·05)	1701 (82·05)				1801 (76·29)
215				0609 (67·62)	1402 (65·68)		1904 (61·14)
216				0609 (67·62)	1403 (55·20)		1902 (55·43)
217	1702 (74·94)	1702 (74·94)	1702 (74·94)				1802 (70·92)
218	0201 (60·57)	1002 (63·07)	3502 (56·06)	0606 (66·11)	1404 (62·19)	2202 (56·95)	2302 (61·85)
219	2001 (65·25)	2001 (65·25)	2102 (69·56)		1404 (62·19)	1903 (64·05)	1903 (64·05)
220	2001 (65·25)	2001 (65·25)	2102 (69·56)	0606 (66·11)	1404 (62·19)	1903 (64·05)	1903 (64·05)
221				4301 (67·17)		4401 (49·26)	4501 (38·68)
222				4301 (67·17)		4401 (49·26)	4501 (38·68)
223							
224	0304 (63·29)	1103 (54·59)	3606 (33·89)		1407 (54·99)	3005 (43·72)	3111 (32·61)

TABLE 6.2

For converting from reference numbers of scale categories to values on the occupation grading scale. The second column contains sequential reference numbers, assigned to categories in the order of their values on the scale, which may be used in place of the reference numbers in the first column.

Category reference number	Sequential category reference number (rank)	Scale value	Category reference number	Sequential category reference number (rank)	Scale value	Category reference number	Sequential category reference number (rank)	Scale value
0101	20	66·24	1601	70	48·51	3107	98	37·60
0102	18	66·86	1701	1	82·05	3108	103	35·67
0103	9	71·72	1702	5	74·94	3109	105	35·53
0104	30	63·75	1703	6	73·06	3110	107	35·03
0201	40	60·57	1704	34	62·33	3111	111	32·61
0301	28	64·04	1801	4	76·29	3112	120	27·23
0302	41	60·12	1802	10	70·92	3201	104	35·55
0303	19	66·45	1803	29	63·88	3202	117	30·00
0304	31	63·29	1901	42	59·38	3203	110	32·67
0401	51	55·53	1902	52	55·43	3204	118	28·35
0402	37	61·68	1903	27	64·05	3301	119	28·33
0403	33	62·83	1904	38	61·14	3302	123	18·36
0404	59	53·92	1905	101	37·14	3401	57	54·28
0501	64	52·35	1906	3	76·71	3402	77	46·62
0601	2	79·53	2001	24	65·25	3403	95	38·96
0602	7	72·19	2101	39	60·89	3501	114	30·78
0603	12	69·14	2102	11	69·56	3502	49	56·06
0604	22	65·85	2201	26	64·30	3601	79	45·94

Code	Rank	Value	Code	Rank	Value	Code	Rank	Value
0605	14	68·66	2202	47	56·95	3602	86	42·70
0606	21	66·11	2203	72	48·15	3603	85	43·25
0607	13	68·98	2301	25	64·84	3604	90	41·18
0608	43	59·23	2302	36	61·85	3605	106	35·24
0609	15	67·62	2303	94	39·85	3606	109	33·89
0701	16	67·24	2304	108	34·62	3701	82	43·98
0801	80	45·58	2401	121	27·10	3702	88	41·43
0901	60	53·87	2402	112	32·42	3703	124	17·52
0902	48	56·50	2501	75	47·32	3801	115	30·05
0903	8	71·74	2601	102	36·05	3901	44	58·15
1001	50	56·02	2701	(category applicable almost entirely to females and not included in the scale)		4001	100	37·18
1002	32	63·07	2801	99	37·44	4002	116	30·01
1101	61	53·85	2901	122	22·95	4101	92	40·92
1102	56	54·59	3001	69	48·55	4201	113	31·49
1103	55	54·59	3002	68	48·91	4301	17	67·17
1201	62	52·89	3003	74	47·49	4401	67	49·26
1202	46	57·24	3004	78	46·51	4501	96	38·68
1203	89	41·25	3005	83	43·72			
1301	91	40·93	3006	87	42·08			
1401	45	57·81	3007	71	48·34			
1402	23	65·68	3008	76	46·80			
1403	53	55·20	3101	93	39·87			
1404	35	62·19	3102	58	54·12			
1405	84	43·40	3103	97	37·62			
1406	63	52·80	3104	65	50·90			
1407	54	54·99	3105	66	50·35			
1501	·73	47·61	3106	81	45·57			

TABLE 6.3

For converting from unit group (rows) and employment status (columns) to sequential category reference number. '125' signifies an impermissible combination of unit group and employment status. Each cell of the table is an occupation grading unit and the entry in a cell is the rank of a category on the scale, employed as a reference number.

Unit Group	Self-employed 25 or more employees 1	Self-employed less than 25 employees 2	Self-employed No employees 3	Manager 25 or more employees 4	Manager less than 25 employees 5	Foreman/ Supervisor 6	Employee 7
001	125	062	082	125	070	071	110
002	044	044	100	044	044	125	125
003	044	044	116	044	044	092	113
004	044	044	116	044	044	092	113
005	059	046	124	080	070	087	118
006	044	044	116	044	044	092	113
007	019	061	085	125	054	071	105
008	037	062	082	125	070	071	110
009	019	061	085	125	054	071	105
010	037	062	082	125	070	071	110
011	125	125	125	125	125	078	104
012	051	062	088	125	070	083	104
013	031	055	090	125	054	083	098
014	031	055	090	125	054	078	098
015	031	055	090	125	054	078	111
016	031	055	090	125	054	078	098
017	051	062	088	125	070	078	104
018	031	055	090	125	054	078	111
019	031	055	090	125	054	083	098
020	031	055	090	125	054	078	111

021	031	055	090	125	054	078	111
022	051	062	088	125	070	078	104
023	051	062	088	125	125	083	104
024	028	056	086	125	054	074	058
025	028	056	106	125	054	074	065
026	125	125	106	125	125	074	103
027	028	056	086	125	054	074	065
028	028	056	086	125	054	074	065
029	051	062	088	125	125	078	104
030	028	056	086	125	054	125	058
031	125	125	125	125	125	078	125
032	125	125	125	125	125	125	098
033	031	055	090	125	054	078	098
034	041	061	085	125	054	076	107
035	031	055	090	125	054	078	098
036	031	055	090	125	054	078	081
037	031	055	090	125	054	068	081
038	031	055	090	125	054	068	098
039	051	062	088	125	125	078	104
040	031	055	090	125	054	068	081
041	028	056	086	125	054	074	065
042	031	055	090	125	054	068	081
043	031	055	090	125	054	068	081
044	031	055	090	125	054	078	111
045	041	061	085	125	054	074	097
046	041	061	085	125	054	074	097
047	051	062	088	125	070	078	104

Unit Group	Self-employed 25 or more employees 1	Self-employed less than 25 employees 2	Self-employed No employees 3	Manager 25 or more employees 4	Manager less than 25 employees 5	Foreman/ Supervisor 6	Employee 7
048	031	055	109	125	054	083	111
049	031	055	086	125	054	069	093
050	031	055	086	125	054	069	093
051	031	055	086	125	054	069	093
052	031	055	090	125	054	078	081
053	125	125	088	125	125	068	104
054	051	062	088	125	070	078	104
055	041	061	085	125	054	068	097
056	031	055	086	125	054	069	093
057	031	055	109	125	054	078	111
058	031	055	090	125	054	068	081
059	031	055	090	125	054	078	111
060	031	055	109	125	054	083	111
061	031	055	090	125	054	078	081
062	031	055	090	125	054	083	111
063	031	055	090	125	054	083	111
064	051	062	088	125	070	083	104
065	051	062	088	125	070	083	104
066	051	062	088	125	070	083	104
067	031	055	109	125	054	083	111
068	031	055	109	125	054	083	111
069	031	055	090	125	054	083	111
070	031	055	109	125	054	083	111
071	031	055	109	125	054	083	111

072	031	055	090	125	054	083	111
073	051	062	088	125	125	083	104
074	031	055	090	125	054	083	111
075	031	055	090	125	054	078	081
076	051	062	088	125	125	083	104
077	031	055	090	125	054	083	111
078	031	055	090	125	054	083	111
079	031	055	090	125	054	083	111
080	031	055	090	125	054	083	111
081	051	062	088	125	070	083	104
082	051	062	088	125	070	083	104
083	031	055	109	125	054	083	111
084	031	055	109	125	054	083	111
085	031	055	090	125	054	069	093
086	031	055	090	125	125	069	098
087	031	055	090	125	054	069	093
088	031	055	090	125	054	069	111
089	031	055	109	125	054	083	111
090	051	062	088	125	070	083	104
091	031	055	090	125	054	068	081
092	051	062	088	125	070	083	104
093	041	061	085	125	054	076	097
094	041	061	085	125	054	076	097
095	041	061	085	125	054	076	097
096	041	061	085	125	054	125	097
097	125	062	082	125	070	076	117
098	033	062	082	125	070	076	117

Unit Group	Self-employed 25 or more employees 1	Self-employed less than 25 employees 2	Self-employed No employees 3	Manager 25 or more employees 4	Manager 25 or less employees 5	Foreman/ Supervisor 6	Employee
099	051	062	088	125	070	083	104
100	041	061	085	125	054	076	097
101	031	055	109	125	054	078	111
102	125	125	125	125	125	083	104
103	125	125	125	125	125	078	107
104	041	061	085	125	054	076	107
105	125	125	125	125	125	078	111
106	125	125	125	125	125	087	118
107	125	125	125	125	125	083	123
108	125	125	125	125	125	083	123
109	125	125	125	125	125	083	123
110	125	125	125	125	125	083	123
111	125	125	125	125	125	083	123
112	125	125	125	125	125	083	123
113	125	091	115	125	125	083	123
114	125	091	115	125	125	076	123
115	020	125	057	022	125	083	125
116	051	062	124	125	125	087	118
117	020	125	057	012	125	125	003
118	125	125	125	125	125	125	103
119	125	125	125	125	125	087	120
120	028	056	106	125	054	125	120
121	028	056	106	125	054	125	120
122	028	056	106	125	054	087	120

123	030	048	125	022	054	101	125
124	125	125	125	125	125	087	103
125	125	125	125	125	054	087	103
126	125	125	125	022	054	026	025
127	125	125	125	125	125	026	121
128	125	125	125	022	125	026	025
129	125	125	125	125	125	087	118
130	125	125	115	125	125	087	123
131	125	125	124	125	125	125	118
132	125	125	125	125	125	087	123
133	064	091	115	125	125	074	119
134	125	125	125	125	125	125	123
135	059	046	124	125	070	087	118
136	059	046	124	080	070	087	118
137	059	046	124	125	125	087	118
138	125	125	125	013	063	125	125
139	040	050	049	125	125	047	094
140	040	050	049	125	125	047	108
141	040	050	049	125	125	047	108
142	125	125	125	125	125	038	125
143	030	048	095	014	063	125	125
144	125	125	125	125	125	072	108
145	125	125	125	125	125	087	118
146	059	089	124	125	073	072	121
147	030	048	077	125	125	125	125
148	040	050	049	125	063	072	094
149	009	008	011	012	063	125	125

Unit Group	Self-employed 25 or more employees 1	Self-employed less than 25 employees 2	Self-employed No employees 3	Manager 25 or more employees 4	Manager less than 25 employees 5	Foreman/ Supervisor 6	Employee 7
150	040	050	114	014	063	072	094
151	125	125	125	015	125	074	065
152	125	125	125	015	125	026	025
153	059	046	124	016	073	072	121
154	020	048	077	043	084	125	125
155	125	125	124	125	125	102	122
156	020	048	095	043	053	125	125
157	125	125	125	043	084	075	075
158	125	125	125	125	125	125	125
159	040	050	114	043	053	125	125
160	125	125	124	125	125	102	122
161	125	125	125	125	125	102	122
162	028	056	106	043	084	099	099
163	125	125	125	125	125	087	123
164	125	125	124	125	125	102	122
165	125	125	125	125	125	072	121
166	064	091	115	125	070	087	123
167	028	056	086	043	084	099	099
168	059	089	124	080	070	087	118
169	028	056	079	043	084	125	066
170	125	125	125	125	125	087	118
171	040	050	114	043	084	125	125
172	125	125	125	125	125	072	112
173	125	125	125	002	125	125	125

174	125	125	125	012	125	125	125
175	125	125	125	021	035	125	125
176	125	125	125	021	035	125	125
177	125	125	125	021	035	125	125
178	125	125	125	021	035	125	125
179	125	125	125	014	063	125	125
180	125	125	125	013	035	125	125
181	001	001	001	125	125	125	004
182	005	005	005	125	125	125	004
183	024	024	011	015	023	038	038
184	006	006	006	125	125	125	010
185	024	024	011	015	023	038	038
186	006	006	006	125	125	125	004
187	024	024	011	015	023	038	038
188	024	024	011	015	023	038	038
189	024	024	011	015	023	038	038
190	125	125	125	015	023	038	038
191	024	024	011	015	023	038	038
192	125	125	125	125	125	125	004
193	024	024	011	015	023	038	038
194	024	024	011	015	023	038	038
195	006	006	006	125	125	125	010
196	006	006	006	125	125	125	010
197	006	006	006	125	125	125	010
198	006	006	006	125	125	125	010
199	024	024	011	021	035	027	027
200	006	006	006	125	125	125	010

Unit Group	Self-employed 25 or more employees 1	Self-employed less than 25 employees 2	Self-employed No employees 3	Manager 25 or more employees 4	Manager less than 25 employees 5	Foreman/ Supervisor 6	Employee 7
201	006	006	006	125	125	125	010
202	006	006	006	125	125	125	010
203	006	006	006	125	125	125	010
204	006	006	006	125	125	125	010
205	006	006	006	125	125	125	010
206	018	060	039	007	045	125	042
207	018	060	039	007	045	125	042
208	018	060	039	007	045	042	042
209	001	001	001	125	125	125	004
210	001	001	001	125	125	125	004
211	006	006	006	125	125	125	004
212	005	005	005	125	125	125	010
213	034	034	034	125	125	125	029
214	001	001	001	125	125	125	004
215	125	125	125	015	023	125	038
216	125	125	125	015	053	125	052
217	005	005	005	125	125	125	010
218	040	032	049	021	035	047	036
219	024	024	011	125	035	027	027
220	024	024	011	021	035	027	027
221	125	125	125	017	125	067	096
222	125	125	125	017	125	067	096
223	125	125	125	125	125	125	125
224	031	055	109	125	054	083	111

Although the sequential reference numbers of the categories are convenient for data-handling purposes, they cannot entirely displace the arbitrary reference numbers since the latter refer to the implicit OPCS classificatory system described in chapter 4 (p. 24). Table 6.5 contains a list of occupation grading units classified by category which, used in conjunction with Appendix B.2 of the *Classification of Occupations, 1970* (see the portion of this Appendix reproduced on p. 25 above), enables the user to map occupation grading units and categories into the superordinate classificatory schemes of the Census (Socio-economic group, Social class, and Socio-economic class)

Table 6.4 contains a convenient summary of the main features of the scale. It does *not* provide guidance on the coding of occupations, which must be undertaken in accordance with the OPCS procedures referred to earlier in this chapter. As we have earlier emphasized, these procedures have been adopted because their employment minimizes the extent to which the coder must resort to the use of his imagination. The Descriptive Titles and lists of occupations in this table are there solely to aid interpretation once the coding has been carried out.

It will be observed that some categories have identical or almost identical scale values. This is a necessary consequence of the limited span which was imposed on the scores of representative occupations by the scoring adjustment described on pp. 55f. The user of the scale who wonders why categories with the same scale value have not been amalgamated without more ado should reflect that employment of the scale values, rounded to the nearest whole number, effects just such an amalgamation; but he should note also that maintaining the distinctions among equal-ranked categories gives him the option of working with situs or other differences which are orthogonal to status differences.

The last two columns of Table 6.4 contain estimates of the frequencies of the categories in the population of employed males aged 20–64 in England and Wales. Which of these estimates is the more reliable is difficult to judge. That derived from a preliminary 1 per cent analysis of the 1971 Census returns has the advantage of a large base (121, 547) and a population which has been completely enumerated, whereas in the case of the Oxford mobility inquiry information is available only for the 83 per cent of men sampled who responded to the inquiry, less the 8½ per cent who were not in full-time employment at the time of the interview. On the other hand, Census data are known to be subject to error resulting from the recording of occupations by householders (Gray and Gee, 1972, p. 104), while in the Oxford mobility inquiry interviewers were extensively briefed in the procedures for eliciting occupational information which are given on pp. 69–72. A further possible source of discrepancies is the different methods of ascertaining size of establishment—indirectly from official records in the case of the Census (see the note on p. 72 above) or directly from a question to the respondent in the Oxford study.

However, the user of the scale will note that, whichever estimate is considered, the frequency with which the scale categories occur in the population is found to vary considerably from category to category. This is a consequence of our principle

(*continued on p. 131*)

TABLE 6.4

The Categories of the scale

Sequential Reference Number (Rank Order)	Reference Number	Descriptive Title* (and occupations of greatest numerical importance)†	Scale Value	% in Oxford Occupational Mobility Sample. (Employed males aged 20–64 resident in England & Wales, 1972. N = 9,457)	% in Employed Male Population of England & Wales aged 20–64 1% Sample Census 1971. N = 121,547
1	1701	Self-employed Professionals I (Doctors; lawyers; accountants)	82·05	0·41	0·35
2	0601	Administrators and Officials I (L) (Senior civil servants)	79·53	0·29	0·28
3	1906	Salaried Professionals I (Airline pilots)	76·71	0·06	0·67
4	1801	Salaried Professionals II (Accountants and company secretaries; doctors; university teachers; opticians)	76·29	1·90	1·59
5	1702	Self-employed Professionals II (Dentists; architects)	74·94	0·20	0·17
6	1703	Self-employed Professionals III (Engineers; surveyors; pharmacists)	73·06	0·23	0·16
7	0602	Administrators and Officials II (L) (Managers in publishing and mass communications)	72·19	0·06	0·03
8	0903	Self-employed Professionals IV (S) (Financial agents; stock and insurance brokers)	71·74	0·01	0·02
9	0103	Self-employed Professionals V (L) (Stock and insurance brokers)	71·72	0·02	0·01

10	1802	Salaried Professionals III (Engineers; natural scientists; architects and town planners)	70·92	3·31	3·12
11	2102	Self-employed Professionals VI (O) (Financial agents)	69·56	0·06	0·05
12	0603	Administrators and Officials III (L) (Local authority senior officers)	69·14	0·39	0·36
13	0607	Administrators and Officials IV (L) (Managers in commerce and public utilities; office managers)	68·98	2·03	1·11
14	0605	Administrators and Officials V (L) (Sales managers)	68·66	1·64	0·80
15	0609	Administrators and Officials VI (L) (Headmasters; senior administrators in social welfare; senior police and fire brigade officers)	67·62	0·40	0·29
16	0701	Administrators and Officials VII (L) (Security officers; managers of security firms)	67·24	0·01	0·01
17	4301	Officers in Armed Services	67·17	0·14	– **
18	0102	Self-employed Professionals VII (L) (Commercial artists)	66·86	0·01	0·00
19	0303	Large Proprietors I (Working owners of mines)	66·45	0·00	0·00
20	0101	Large Proprietors II (Proprietors of hotels, boarding houses, and inns)	66·24	0·01	0·00

Sequential Reference Number (Rank Order)	Reference Number	Descriptive Title* (and occupations of greatest numerical importance)†	Scale Value	% in Oxford Occupational Mobility Sample. (Employed males aged 20–64 resident in England & Wales, 1972. N = 9,457)	% in Employed Male Population of England & Wales aged 20–64 1% Sample Census 1971. N = 121,547
21	0606	Industrial and Business Managers I (L) (Managers in engineering, extraction industries, general manufacturing and construction; personnel managers)	66·11	1·95	1·29
22	0604	Industrial and Business Managers II (L) (Managers in transport and communications)	65·85	0·14	0·11
23	1402	Administrators and Officials VIII (S) (Headmasters; managers in social welfare)	65·68	0·14	0·02
24	2001	Self-employed Professionals VIII (Chiropodists; physiotherapists; private teachers and tutors)	65·25	0·05	0·02
25	2301	Administrators and Officials IX (Traffic controllers; telegraph and radio officers; police officers)	64·84	0·73	0·74
26	2201	Administrators and Officials X (Superintendents in telephone exchanges; police sergeants)	64·30	0·17	0·12
27	1903	Technicians I (Senior laboratory technicians; senior work study and progress engineers)	64·05	1·63	1·94
28	0301	Large Proprietors III (Hauliers; coach proprietors)	64·04	0·01	0·00

29	1803	Salaried Professionals IV (Non-parochial clergy, ministers of religion)	63·88	0·05	0·05
30	0104	Large Proprietors IV (Shop and store proprietors; garage proprietors)	63·75	0·15	0·01
31	0304	Large Proprietors V (Working owners of metal working firms)	63·29	0·05	0·00
32	1002	Small Proprietors I (Working owners of industrial design firms)	63·07	0·00	0·00
33	0403	Large Proprietors VI (Working owners of demolition and specialist construction firms)	62·83	0·01	0·00
34	1704	Self-employed Professionals IX (Parochial clergy)	62·33	0·20	0·17
35	1404	Industrial and Business Managers III (S) (Managers in commerce, public utilities, engineering, extraction industries, general manufacturing and construction; personnel managers)	62·19	0·87	2·41
36	2302	Technicians II (Draughtsmen; technical illustrators)	61·85	0·80	0·90
37	0402	Large Proprietors VII (Working owners of quarries)	61·68	0·00	0·00
38	1904	Salaried Professionals V (Primary and secondary school teachers; civil service executive officers; social welfare workers; male nurses; public health inspectors)	61·14	3·11	2·64

Sequential Reference Number (Rank Order)	Reference Number	Descriptive Title* (and occupations of greatest numerical importance)†	Scale Value	% in Oxford Occupational Mobility Sample. (Employed males aged 20–64 resident in England & Wales, 1972. N = 9,457	% in Employed Male Population of England & Wales aged 20–64 1% Sample Census 1971. N = 121,547
39	2101	Self-employed Professionals X (O) (Entertainers; artists; journalists)	60·89	0·15	0·16
40	0201	Large Proprietors VIII (Estate agents; travel agents; auctioneers)	60·57	0·03	0·01
41	0302	Large Proprietors IX (Working owners of building, joinery, plumbing and painting and decorating firms)	60·12	0·08	0·00
42	1901	Salaried Professionals VI (Journalists; commercial artists)	59·38	0·37	0·32
43	0608	Managers in Services I (L) (Hotel and restaurant managers)	59·23	0·15	0·10
44	3901	Farmers and Farm Managers	58·15	0·86	0·79
45	1401	Managers in Services II (S) (Managers in journalism; theatre and ballroom managers)	57·81	0·05	0·06
46	1202	Small Proprietors II (Landscape and other gardeners)	57·24	0·03	0·01
47	2202	Supervisors of Nonmanual Employees I (Supervisors of clerical employees)	56·95	0·95	0·41
48	0902	Small Proprietors III (Boarding house proprietors; publicans; garage proprietors; coach proprietors)	56·50	1·19	1·09
49	3502	Small Proprietors IV (O) (Lodging house proprietors; wholesalers)	56·06	0·10	0·15

50	1001	Small Proprietors V (Restaurant and café proprietors)	56·02	0·31	0·30
51	0401	Large Proprietors X (Boat proprietors; warehouse proprietors)	55·53	0·00	0·00
52	1902	Managers in Services III (Officials of occupational, trade, and political organizations)	55·43	0·06	0·03
53	1403	Managers in Services IV (S) (Managers of hotels, boarding houses, restaurants, and cafés)	55·20	0·06	0·16
54	1407	Managers in Services V (S) (Managers of shops and service agencies)	54·99	0·21	0·23
55	1103	Small Proprietors VI (Working owners of metal-working firms; butchers; bakers; shoe-makers; cabinet-makers; printers; tailors; upholsterers)	54·59	0·60	0·31
56	1102	Small Proprietors VII (Electricians; auto-engineers; taxi firm proprietors; hauliers)	54·59	0·34	0·28
57	3401	Small Proprietors VIII (O) (Boat proprietors)	54·28	0·00	0·02
58	3102	Technicians III (Electrical, radar, and radio engineers)	54·12	0·33	0·38
59	0404	Large Proprietors XI (Warehouse proprietors)	53·92	0·01	0·00
60	0901	Small Proprietors IX (Theatre proprietors; commercial artists)	53·87	0·04	0·03

Sequential Reference Number (Rank Order)	Reference Number	Descriptive Title* (and occupations of greatest numerical importance)†	Scale Value	% in Oxford Occupational Mobility Sample. (Employed males aged 20–64 resident in England & Wales, 1972. N = 9,457	% in Employed Male Population of England & Wales aged 20–64 1% Sample Census 1971. N = 121,547
61	1101	Small Proprietors X (Builders; painters and decorators; plumbers)	53·85	0·96	0·43
62	1201	Small Proprietors XI (Working owners of textile firms; specialist construction firms)	52·89	0·16	0·13
63	1406	Managers in Services VI (S) (Office managers in commerce and distribution)	52·80	1·51	2·44
64	0501	Large Proprietors XII (Working owners of office and industrial cleaning firms)	52·35	0·00	0·00
65	3104	Technicians IV (Electrical and electronics fitters; Post Office technicians; auto-engineers)	50·90	3·51	3·28
66	3105	Salaried Professionals VII (Professional athletes and sportsmen)	50·35	0·04	0·03
67	4401	Non-Commissioned Officers in Armed Services	49·26	0·18	— **
68	3002	Supervisors of Manual Employees (Manuf.) I (Foremen in toolrooms, maintenance departments, fitting shops)	48·91	1·34	0·54
69	3001	Supervisors of Manual Employees (Manuf.) II (Foremen in printing, watch- and instrument-making)	48·55	0·13	0·11

70	1601	Managers in Services VII (S) (Warehouse managers)	48·51	0·10	0·14
71	3007	Supervisors of Manual Employees (F.M. & Q) (Colliery under-officials)	48·34	0·22	0·21
72	2203	Supervisors of Nonmanual Employees II (Supervisors of sales personnel)	48·15	0·44	0·26
73	1501	Managers in Services VIII (S) (Managers of mobile shops, market stalls)	47·61	0·00	0·01
74	3003	Supervisors of Manual Employees (Manuf.) III (Foremen electricians and plumbers; foremen in garages; dock foremen)	47·49	1·00	0·49
75	2501	Service Workers I (Stewards; hostel superintendents)	47·32	0·00	0·01
76	3008	Supervisors of Manual Employees (Const.) (Foremen in civil engineering, building and earth-moving firms)	46·80	0·95	0·55
77	3402	Self-employed Workers I (O) (Publicans; garage owners)	46·62	0·06	0·15
78	3004	Supervisors of Manual Employees (Manuf.) IV (Foremen in engineering; foremen in gasworks, shipyards, blast furnaces, and sawmills)	46·51	1·00	0·87
79	3601	Self-employed Workers II (O) (Athletes, sportsmen, coaches)	45·94	0·02	0·01
80	0801	Managers in Services IX (L) (Warehouse managers; laundry managers)	45·58	0·17	0·11
81	3106	Skilled Manual Workers (Manuf.) I (Maintenance and other fitters; millwrights; toolmakers; pattern-makers)	45·57	5·20	5·89

Sequential Reference Number (Rank Order)	Reference Number	Descriptive Title* (and occupations of greatest numerical importance)†	Scale Value	% in Oxford Occupational Mobility Sample. (Employed males aged 20–64 resident in England & Wales, 1972. N = 9,457	% in Employed Male Population of England & Wales aged 20–64 1% Sample Census 1971. N = 121,547
82	3701	Self-employed Workers III (O) (Fishermen; construction site workers)	43·98	0·26	0·29
83	3005	Supervisors of Manual Employees (Manuf.) V (Foremen in metal working plants, chemical plants, textile factories, brickyards, potteries, glass works, tanneries, food processing plants; foremen over labourers)	43·72	0·93	0·75
84	1405	Managers in Services X (S) (Managers of hotels, bars, ballrooms, baths)	43·40	0·24	0·21
85	3603	Self-employed Workers IV (O) (Plumbers; carpenters and joiners; jobbing builders; painters and decorators)	43·25	1·32	1·55
86	3602	Self-employed Workers V (O) (Electricians; watch repairers; jewellery makers; hairdressers)	42·70	0·29	0·38
87	3006	Supervisors of Manual Employees (T.C. & S.) I (Supervisors and foremen in postal services, warehousing and distribution; petty officers in Merchant Navy)	42·08	1·22	0·49
88	3702	Self-employed Workers VI (O) (Metal workers)	41·43	0·01	0·05
89	1203	Small Proprietors XII (Proprietors of laundries and dry cleaning shops, mobile shops, market stalls)	41·25	0·08	0·04

90	3604	Self-employed Workers VII (O) (Butchers; shoemakers; tailors; upholsterers)	41·18	0·26	0·31
91	1301	Small Proprietors XIII (Working owners of office and industrial cleaning firms; window cleaners)	40·93	0·02	0·04
92	4101	Supervisors in Agriculture	40·92	0·16	0·08
93	3101	Skilled Manual Workers (Manuf.) II (Printers, compositors, precision instrument makers)	39·87	0·90	0·85
94	2303	Nonmanual Employees (Clerical workers; cashiers; commercial travellers)	39·85	6·46	7·68
95	3403	Self-employed Workers VIII (O) (Shopkeepers; miscellaneous dealers and traders; boarding-house keepers)	38·96	0·76	0·87
96	4501	Other Ranks in Armed Services	38·68	0·16	—**
97	3103	Skilled Manual Workers (Const.) I (Carpenters and joiners; painters and decorators; bricklayers)	37·62	4·41	4·04
98	3107	Skilled Manual Workers (Manuf.) III (Machine setters; sheetmetal workers; rolling and tube mill operators; glass and ceramic formers)	37·60	2·82	2·70
99	2801	Service Workers II (Cooks)	37·44	0·38	0·38
100	4001	Smallholders (O)	37·18	0·73	0·72

Sequential Reference Number (Rank Order)	Reference Number	Descriptive Title* (and occupations of greatest numerical importance)†	Scale Value	% in Oxford Occupational Mobility Sample. (Employed males aged 20–64 resident in England & Wales, 1972. N = 9,457	% in Employed Male Population of England & Wales aged 20–64 1% Sample Census 1971. N = 121,547
101	1905	Supervisors of Manual Employees (T.C. & S.) II (Supervisors and inspectors in road and rail transport)	37·14	0·23	0·21
102	2601	Service Workers III (Head waiters; head barmen; canteen superintendents)	36·05	0·10	0·11
103	3108	Skilled Manual Workers (T.C. & S.) I (Engine drivers; signalmen)	35·67	0·48	0·55
104	3201	Semi-skilled Manual Workers (Manuf.) I (Machine tool operators; press operators; assemblers and routine inspectors; chemical process workers; food and other process workers)	35·55	6·02	6·33
105	3109	Skilled Manual Workers (F.M. & Q.) (Coalminers)	35·53	0·90	1·15
106	3605	Self-employed Workers IX (O) (Taxi drivers; carriers)	35·24	0·48	0·33
107	3110	Skilled Manual Workers (Const.) II (Operators of cranes and earth-moving equipment)	35·03	1·39	1·14
108	2304	Service Workers IV (Shop salesmen and assistants)	34·62	0·54	1·03

109	3606	Self-employed Workers X (O) (Metal-working craftsmen)	33·89	0·04	0·02
110	3203	Semi-skilled Manual Workers (F.M. & Q.) I (Surface workers at coalmines; quarry workers)	32·67	0·27	0·31
111	3111	Skilled Manual Workers (Manuf.) IV (Plant and engine operators; locksmiths, engravers and other metal-working craftsmen; moulders, furnacemen and forgemen; sawyers and woodworkers; butchers; bakers)	32·61	5·02	4·97
112	2402	Service Workers V (Photographers; cinema projectionists; baths attendants; doormen; commissioners)	32·42	0·39	0·36
113	4201	Agricultural Workers	31·49	1·56	1·22
114	3501	Self-employed Workers XI (O) (Café and snack-bar owners)	30·78	0·17	0·21
115	3801	Self-employed Workers XII (O) (Window cleaners; sweeps)	30·05	0·15	0·26
116	4002	Self-employed Workers XIII (O) (Hedgers; ditchers; turf-cutters)	30·01	0·06	0·08
117	3202	Semi-skilled Manual Workers (Const.) I (Roofers; asphalters; bricklayers' labourers; demolition workers)	30·00	1·79	1·07
118	3204	Semi-skilled Manual Workers (T.C. & S.) I (Warehousemen; packers and labellers; storekeepers; postal workers; roundsmen; ambulance men; deckhands; railway lengthmen; gardeners and groundsmen)	28·35	5·16	5·28

Sequential Reference Number (Rank Order)	Reference Number	Descriptive Title* (and occupations of greatest numerical importance)†	Scale Value	% in Oxford Occupational Mobility Sample. (Employed males aged 20–64 resident in England & Wales, 1972. N = 9,457	% in Employed Male Population of England & Wales aged 20–64 1% Sample Census 1971. N = 121,547
119	3301	Unskilled Manual Workers I (Dock labourers)	28·33	0·25	0·24
120	3112	Skilled Manual Workers (T.C. & S.) II (Lorry, bus, and coach drivers)	27·23	4·64	4·88
121	2401	Service Workers VI (Caretakers; guards and attendants; telephone operators)	27·10	1·14	1·33
122	2901	Service Workers VII (Waiters; barmen; counter hands)	22·95	0·17	0·38
123	3302	Unskilled Manual Workers II (General labourers; factory labourers; building site labourers; railway porters; kitchen porters; office and industrial cleaners; messengers)	18·36	3·12	6·11
124	3703	Self-employed Workers XIV (O) (Street vendors; jobbing gardeners)	17·52	0·31	0·23
				99·94	98·57**

* These titles are not in strict correspondence with the titles of any OPCS occupational categories, such as the Socio-economic groups. They are intended to serve a descriptive purpose only and should in no circumstances be taken as providing a frame for the coding of occupations. The letters in brackets following a title provide information on the employment status of occupations making up the category which may not be evident from the descriptive title.

(L) = Large: i.e. establishments with 25 or more employees
(S) = Small: i.e. establishments with less than 25 employees
(O) = Self-employed without employees

The following abbreviations are also used to indicate economic sector:

Manuf.   = Manufacturing
F.M. & Q. = Fishing, Mining, and Quarrying
Const.   = Construction
T.C. & S.   = Transport, Communications and Services

† Based on data from the 1971 1 per cent Sample Census. To determine the full range of titles covered by a category it is necessary to work back from its reference number to its constituent OPCS unit groups (see above p. 95). Note that the same occupation titles may be given for two or more categories, where these are associated with different employment statuses.

** Officers, NCOs and Other Ranks in the armed forces are assigned, respectively, to categories 17, 67, and 96. The Census makes no distinction among ranks and so the 1·49 per cent of the Sample Census who are in the armed services cannot be distributed among the three categories.

TABLE 6.5

Occupation grading units (i.e. permissible combinations of unit group and employment status) classified by category. The codes of the unit groups are those given in the Classification of Occupations, 1970 (OPCS). The employment status codes are those given in Table 4.1

Category reference number	Unit group	Employment status
0101	115	1
	117	1
	154	1
	156	1
0102	206	1
	207	1
	208	1
0103	149	1
0104	123	1
	143	1
	147	1
0201	139	1
	140	1
	141	1
	148	1
	150	1
	159	1
	171	1
	218	1
0301	024	1
	025	1

Category reference number	Unit group	Employment status
0304	019	1
	020	1
	021	1
	033	1
	035	1
	036	1
	037	1
	038	1
	040	1
	042	1
	043	1
	044	1
	048	1
	049	1
	050	1
	051	1
	052	1
	056	1
	057	1
	058	1
	059	1

0401

060 061 062 063 067 068 069 070 071 072 074 075 077 078 079 080 083 084 085 086 087 088 089 091 101 224 012

1 1 1 1 1 1 1 1 1 1 1 1 1 1 1 1 1 1 1 1 1 1 1 1 1 1 1

0302

0303

0304

027 028 030 041 120 121 122 162 167 169 034 045 046 055 093 094 095 096 100 104 007 009 013 014 015 016 018

1 1 1 1 1 1 1 1 1 1 1 1 1 1 1 1 1 1 1 1 1 1 1 1 1 1 1

Catgory reference number	Unit group	Employment status	Category reference number	Unit group	Employment status
0401	017	1	0607	180	4
	022	1	0608	154	4
	023	1		156	4
	029	1		157	4
	039	1		159	4
	047	1		162	4
	054	1		167	4
	064	1		169	4
	065	1		171	4
	066	1	0609	151	4
	073	1		152	4
	076	1		183	4
	081	1		185	4
	082	1		187	4
	090	1		188	4
	092	1		189	4
	099	1		190	4
	116	1		191	4
0402	008	1		193	4
	010	1		194	4
0403	098	1		215	4
0404	005	1		216	4
	135	1	0701	153	4
	136	1	0801	005	4
	137	1		136	4

Code	No.	Val
0501	146	1
	153	1
	168	1
	133	1
	166	1
0601	173	4
0602	206	4
	207	4
	208	4
0603	117	4
	149	4
	174	4
0604	115	4
	123	4
	126	4
	128	4
0605	143	4
	150	4
	179	4
0606	175	4
	176	4
	177	4
	178	4
	199	4
	218	4
	220	4
0607	138	4

Code	No.	Val
0901	168	4
	206	2
	207	2
	208	2
0902	123	2
	143	2
	147	2
	154	2
	156	2
0903	149	2
1001	139	2
	140	2
	141	2
	148	2
	150	2
	159	2
	171	2
	218	2
1002	007	2
1101	009	2
	034	2
	045	2
	046	2
	055	2
	093	2
	094	2
	095	2

Category reference number	Unit group	Employment status	Category reference number	Unit group	Employment status
1101	096	2	1103	075	2
	100	2		077	2
	104	2		078	2
1102	024	2		079	2
	025	2		080	2
	027	2		083	2
	028	2		084	2
	030	2		085	2
	041	2		086	2
	120	2		087	2
	121	2		088	2
	122	2		089	2
	162	2		091	2
	167	2		101	2
	169	2		224	2
1103	013	2	1201	001	2
	014	2		008	2
	015	2		010	2
	016	2		012	2
	018	2		017	2
	019	2		022	2
	020	2		023	2
	021	2		029	2
	033	2		039	2
	035	2		047	2

054		2
064		2
065		2
066		2
073		2
076		2
081		2
082		2
090		2
092		2
097		2
098		2
099		2
116	1202	2
005		2
135		2
136	1203	2
137	1301	2
153		2
146		2
168	1401	2
113		2
114		2
133		2
166		2
206		5
207		5

036	2
037	2
038	2
040	2
042	2
043	2
044	2
048	2
049	2
050	2
051	2
052	2
056	2
057	2
058	2
059	2
060	2
061	2
062	2
063	2
067	2
068	2
069	2
070	2
071	2
072	2
074	2

Category Reference number	Unit group	Employment status
1401	208	5
1402	183	5
	185	5
	187	5
	188	5
	189	5
	190	5
	191	5
	193	5
	194	5
	215	5
1403	156	5
	159	5
	216	5
1404	175	5
	176	5
	177	5
	178	5
	180	5
	199	5
	218	5
	219	5
	220	5
1405	154	5
	157	5

Category reference number	Unit group	Employment status
1407	035	5
	036	5
	037	5
	038	5
	040	5
	041	5
	042	5
	043	5
	044	5
	045	5
	046	5
	048	5
	049	5
	050	5
	051	5
	052	5
	055	5
	056	5
	057	5
	058	5
	059	5
	060	5
	061	5
	062	5
	063	5

	5	5	5	5	5	5	5	5	5	5	5	5	5	5	5	5	5	5	5	5	5	5	5	5	5	5	5
	067	068	069	070	071	072	074	075	077	078	079	080	083	084	085	087	088	089	091	093	094	095	096	100	101	104	120

	5	5	5	5	5	5	5	5	5	5	5	5	5	5	5	5	5	5	5	5	5	5	5	5	5	5	5
	162	167	169	171	138	143	148	149	150	179	007	009	013	014	015	016	018	019	020	021	024	025	027	028	030	033	034

1406

1407

Category reference number	Unit group	Employment status
1407	121	5
	122	5
	123	5
	125	5
	126	5
	224	5
1501	146	5
	153	5
1601	001	5
	005	5
	008	5
	010	5
	012	5
	017	5
	022	5
	047	5
	054	5
	064	5
	065	5
	066	5
	081	5
	082	5
	090	5
	092	5
	097	5

Category reference number	Unit group	Employment status
1703	184	1
	184	2
	184	3
	186	1
	186	2
	186	3
	195	1
	195	2
	195	3
	196	1
	196	2
	196	3
	197	1
	197	2
	197	3
	198	1
	198	2
	198	3
	200	1
	200	2
	200	3
	201	1
	201	2
	201	3
	202	1

1701	098	5
	099	5
	135	5
	136	5
	166	5
	168	5
	181	1
	181	2
	181	3
	209	1
	209	2
	209	3
	210	1
	210	2
	210	3
	214	1
	214	2
	214	3
1702	182	1
	182	2
	182	3
	212	1
	212	2
	212	3
	217	1
	217	2
	217	3

	202	2
	202	3
	203	1
	203	2
	203	3
	204	1
	204	2
	204	3
	205	1
	205	2
	205	3
	211	1
	211	2
	211	3
1704	213	1
	213	2
	213	3
1801	181	7
	182	7
	186	7
	192	7
	209	7
	210	7
	211	7
	214	7
1802	184	7
	195	7

Category reference number	Unit group	Employment status	Category reference number	Unit group	Employment status
1802	196	7	2001	189	2
	197	7		191	1
	198	7		191	2
	200	7		193	1
	201	7		193	2
	202	7		194	1
	203	7		194	2
	204	7		199	1
	205	7		199	2
	212	7		219	1
	217	7		219	2
1803	213	7		220	1
1901	206	7		220	2
	207	6	2101	206	3
	208	7		207	3
	208	7		208	3
1902	216	7	2102	149	3
1903	199	6		183	3
	199	7		185	3
	219	6		187	3
	219	7		188	3
	220	6		189	3
	220	7		191	3
1904	142	6		193	3
	183	6		194	3

1905	183	7	2201	199	3
1906	185	6		219	3
2001	185	7		220	3
	187	6	2202	126	6
	187	7		127	6
	188	6		128	6
	188	7	2203	152	6
	189	6		139	6
	189	7		140	6
	190	6		141	6
	190	7		218	6
	191	6		144	6
	191	7		146	6
	193	7		148	6
	194	7		150	6
	215	7		153	6
	123	6	2301	165	6
	117	7		172	6
	183	1	2302	126	7
	183	2	2303	128	7
	185	1		152	7
	185	2		218	7
	187	1	2304	139	7
	187	2		148	7
	188	1		150	7
	188	2		140	7
	189	1		141	7

122

Category reference number	Unit group	Employment status
2304	144	7
2401	127	7
	146	7
	153	7
	165	7
2402	172	7
2501	157	6
	157	7
2601	155	6
	160	6
	161	6
	164	6
2701	158	7
2801	162	6
	162	7
	167	6
	167	7
2901	155	7
	160	7
	161	7
	164	7
3001	049	6
	050	6
	051	6
	056	6

Category reference number	Unit group	Employment status
3004	017	6
	018	6
	020	6
	021	6
	022	6
	029	6
	031	6
	033	6
	035	6
	036	6
	039	6
	044	6
	047	6
	052	6
	054	6
	057	6
	059	6
	061	6
	075	6
	101	6
	103	6
3005	105	6
	012	6
	013	6
	019	6

6 6 6 6 6 6 6 6 6 6 6 6 6 6 6 6 6 6 6 6 6 6 6 6 6 6 6

023 048 060 062 063 064 065 066 067 068 069 070 071 072 073 074 076 077 078 079 080 081 082 083 084 089 090

6 6 6 6 6 6 6 6 6 6 6 6 6 6 6 6 6 6 6 6 6 6 6 6 6 6 6

085 086 087 088 037 038 040 042 043 053 055 058 091 024 025 026 027 028 041 045 046 133 151 011 014 015 016

3002

3003

3004

Category reference number	Unit group	Employment states	Category reference number	Unit group	Employment status
3005	092	6	3103	046	7
	099	6		055	7
	102	6		093	7
	107	6		094	7
	108	6		095	7
	109	6		096	7
	110	6		100	7
	111	6	3104	025	7
	112	6		027	7
	114	6		028	7
	224	6		041	7
3006	005	6		151	7
	106	6	3105	169	7
	116	6	3106	036	7
	119	6		037	7
	122	6		040	7
	124	6		042	7
	125	6		043	7
	129	6		052	7
	130	6		058	7
	132	6		061	7
	135	6		075	7
	136	6		091	7
	137	6	3107	013	7
	145	6		014	7

		7 7 7 7 7 7 7 7 7 7 7 7 7 7 7 7 7 7 7 7 7 7 7 7 7 7 7

Group	Numbers	Code
	016	7
	019	7
	032	7
	033	7
	035	7
	038	7
	086	7
3108	026	7
	118	7
	124	7
	125	7
3109	007	7
	009	7
3110	034	7
	103	7
	104	7
3111	015	7
	018	7
	020	7
	021	7
	044	7
	048	7
	057	7
	059	7
	060	7
	062	7
	063	7

Group	Numbers	Code
3007	163	6
	166	6
	168	6
	170	6
3008	001	6
	007	6
	008	6
	009	6
	010	6
	034	6
	093	6
	094	6
	095	6
	097	6
	098	6
	100	6
	104	6
	113	6
3101	049	7
	050	7
	051	7
	056	7
	085	7
	087	7
3102	024	7
	030	7
3103	045	7

126

Category reference number	Unit group	Employment status
3111	067	7
	068	7
	069	7
	070	7
	071	7
	072	7
	074	7
	077	7
	078	7
	079	7
	080	7
	083	7
	084	7
	088	7
	089	7
	101	7
	105	7
	224	7
3112	119	7
	120	7
	121	7
	122	7
3201	011	7
	012	7
	017	7

Category reference number	Unit group	Employment status
3204	131	7
	135	7
	136	7
	137	7
	145	7
	168	7
	170	7
3301	133	7
3302	107	7
	108	7
	109	7
	110	7
	111	7
	112	7
	113	7
	114	7
	130	7
	132	7
	134	7
	163	7
	166	7
3401	115	3
	117	3
3402	147	3
	154	3

022		7	3403	143	3
023		7	3501	156	3
029		7		150	3
039		7		159	3
047		7	3502	171	3
053		7		139	3
054		7		140	3
064		7		141	3
065		7		148	3
066		7	3601	218	3
073		7	3602	169	3
076		7		024	3
081		7		027	3
082		7		028	3
090		7		030	3
092		7		041	3
099		7		049	3
102		7		050	3
097	3202	7		051	3
098		7		056	3
001	3203	7	3603	167	3
008		7		007	3
010	3204	7		009	3
005		7		034	3
106		7		045	3
116		7		046	3
129		7		055	3

Category reference number	Unit group	Employment status
3603	093	3
	094	3
	095	3
	096	3
	100	3
	104	3
3604	013	3
	014	3
	015	3
	016	3
	018	3
	019	3
	020	3
	021	3
	033	3
	035	3
	036	3
	037	3
	038	3
	040	3
	042	3
	043	3
	044	3
	052	3
	058	3

Category reference number	Unit group	Employment status
3606	068	3
	070	3
	071	3
	083	3
	084	3
	089	3
	101	3
	224	3
3701	001	3
	008	3
	010	3
	097	3
	098	3
3702	012	3
	017	3
	022	3
	023	3
	029	3
	039	3
	047	3
	053	3
	054	3
	064	3
	065	3
	066	3

073	3	
076	3	
081	3	
082	3	
090	3	
092	3	
099	3	
005	3	
116	3	3703
131	3	
135	3	
136	3	
137	3	
146	3	
153	3	
155	3	
160	3	
164	3	3801
168	3	
113	3	
114	3	
130	3	3901
133	3	
166	3	
002	1	
002	2	
002	4	

059	3	
061	3	
062	3	
063	3	
069	3	
072	3	
074	3	
075	3	
077	3	
078	3	
079	3	
080	3	
085	3	
086	3	
087	3	
088	3	
091	3	
025	3	
026	3	
120	3	3605
121	3	
122	3	
162	3	3606
048	3	
057	3	
060	3	
067	3	

Category reference number	Unit group	Employment status
3901	002	5
	003	1
	003	2
	003	4
	003	5
	004	1
	004	2
	004	4
	004	5
	006	1
	006	2
	006	4
	006	5
4001	002	3
4002	003	3

Category reference number	Unit group	Employment status
4002	004	3
	006	3
4101	003	6
	004	6
	006	6
4201	003	7
	004	7
	006	7
4301	221	4
	222	4
4401	221	6
	222	6
4501	221	7
	222	7

of attempting to achieve the greatest and most uniform degree of intra-category homogeneity consistent with the extent of heterogeneity inherent in the constituent occupation grading units. There is little to be gained from the disaggregation of a numerically large category if in fact all occupations in that category are of very similar standing.

The mean scale value of the men in the Oxford mobility enquiry is 44·87, the standard deviation is 14·78 and the median is 39·8. Although the scale values are given to two decimal places in Tables 6.1, 6.2, and 6.4, for many purposes it will be sufficient to round them to the nearest whole number.

The exposition of the procedures of the scale is now complete. The remaining sections of this chapter are intended as 'additional notes' to users of the scale on the matters of (i) collapsing the scale; (ii) interpreting the scale; and (iii) nomenclature. We do of course hope that the advice and recommendations which they contain will be generally accepted by users; but the issues that arise are ones on which ultimately each user must be free to rely on his own judgement.

Collapsing the scale

A major objective in constructing the scale was to provide a means of giving to any occupation, as typically engaged in by a male, a numerical value which could be interpreted as a measure, subject to estimable error, of the 'general desirability' of that occupation. It must be understood that something will inevitably be lost if the scale is not retained in its complete form. Nevertheless, some users may still have good reason for wishing to reduce the 124 categories to some more manageable number, and in recognition of this fact, a 36-category version of the scale is presented in Table 6.6. The principles according to which this collapse was made were the following:*

(1) No amalgamations of categories were made across *major* employment status divisions—i.e. those of employer/manager/employee. In some few cases, 'supervisory' categories were combined with either managerial categories (small establishments) or employee categories,[†] and self-employed categories (without employees) with employer (small establishments) categories.

(2) No amalgamations of categories were made across broad occupational divisions such as those of professionals, technicians, nonmanual, and manual workers; and, in the case of the latter, major sectorial divisions were preserved.

(3) Within the constraints set by (1) and (2), amalgamations were made of categories adjacent to each other in the ordering of the complete scale. In the large majority of cases, the collapsed categories have a range of less than 5 scale points, but in some few instances the range was extended beyond this to enable a collapse to take in a numerically very small category which would otherwise have been isolated.

* The precise nature of the collapse can, of course, be ascertained by comparing the
  column of 'Constituent categories' in Table 6.6 with Table 6.4
† As indeed they already are in some of the implicit OPCS groupings on which our scale is
  founded.

(4) The positioning of dividing lines between the collapsed categories (apart from those required by (1) and (2)) was determined by the occurence of obvious 'breaks' in the scale values of the original categories or, if no such break was apparent, by inspection of the patterns of intergenerational mobility between categories revealed in a 124 × 124 father-son mobility matrix; i.e. dividing lines were drawn so as to place together those categories showing the greatest amounts of intergenerational 'exchange' of personnel.

It is not pretended that the collapse of the scale represented by Table 6.6 will suit the purposes of all users; for instance, a study of a local labour market dominated by a small number of industries would probably call for a quite different rearrangement of the 124 categories. However, the collapse suggested has already proved its value in our analysis of occupational mobility among a large sample of the male population aged 20—64 in England and Wales, and we commend it to the consideration of the research worker who is studying a broadly comparable population.

Finally in this connection we would urge, in the interests of the comparability of data, that *whatever* modifications users may make to the categories of our scale, they should clearly specify the procedures they have followed so that other investigators can replicate them, if necessary by returning to the basic occupation grading units (Table 6.5) and assembling these according to explicit rules.

Interpreting the scale

In chapter 2 (and Appendix A) we have already argued at some length against taking the results of 'occupational prestige' studies at face value—i.e. as tapping some underlying structure of social relations of deference, acceptance and derogation—and in favour of an alternative interpretation of these data in terms of the 'general desirability' of occupations, understood as a synthetic, emergent judgement from a specific population. It remains here to make only two further points.

First, it must be emphasized that it is entirely possible for anyone unconvinced by our arguments to regard and use our scale as one of occupational prestige in the conventional sense. There is nothing whatsoever in the construction of the scale to prevent this. In particular, it should be remembered that the criterion by which respondents in the national grading enquiry were asked to rank occupations was that of their 'social standing'; that is, the criterion which investigators of occupational prestige, as conventionally understood, have themselves tended most often to use.

Secondly, it must be made clear that if, on the other hand, our own interpretation of the scale is accepted, then it follows from this that no inferences should be drawn from the position, or movement, of individuals or groups on the scale to their social experience and behaviour (in terms, say, of their patterns of intimate association or life-styles) or to their social values and attitudes. In place of such inferences, there must be specific empirical inquiry. For example, in the case of mobility studies, the investigator ought not, on our argument, to take occupational level as measured by our scale, as a variable which can serve as some kind of all-purpose indicator of the position of an individual or group across the several dimensions of social stratification. He should, rather, treat the connections between mobility (or stability) in occupational level and the experience of relational or subcultural discontinuity or shifts in behavioural patterns, social values and attitudes, etc. *as issues to be independently investigated.* In other words, while we believe that our scale, understood as one of the 'general desirability' of occupations in popular assessment, can serve in itself as a valuable measuring-rod in studies of occupational achievement and occupational mobility *per se*, it is not, in our interpretation of it, one which entails any assumptions about specific extra-occupational consequences which follow from holding, or moving between, given occupational levels. For the investigator whose concern is with such consequences, what it provides is a basis from which systematic inquiry may proceed.

Nomenclature

It should be evident that the procedures described in this monograph—the manifold classificatory schemes which have been constructed, and the complex methods of ensuring that each scheme can be mapped strictly into others—could lead to confusion if users fail to employ them systematically. Furthermore, the intelligibility of tables and research reports will be seriously impaired if the precise principle of organization employed in the data which they present is not uniquely identified. We therefore set out here the terms which we have employed in using the procedures of the monograph in the work of the Oxford occupational mobility inquiry, with a recommendation that other workers should use them with exactly the reference that we have given to them (and that, if they adapt our procedures to their own purposes, they should employ distinct terms of their own).

When a man is projected on to the scale and assigned a number from 18 to 82 (cf. the scale values in Table 6.2) we refer to this as his *Hope-Goldthorpe scale value* or *H-G value* for short. The scale we refer to as the *Hope-Goldthorpe scale* and abbreviate it similarly. When a man is assigned to one or other of the categories, this is referred to as his *Hope-Goldthorpe category* (there is no need to specify explicitly whether arbitrary or sequential reference numbers are used to denominate the categories since the former all have four digits and the latter have three digits). If a user, to fulfil his own purposes, computes H-G scale values and then collapses these into, let us say, five-point intervals, it is strongly urged that he should refer to these as 'intervals' and *not* as 'categories'. To insist on this distinction is not mere pedantry since the possibility of employing principles of categorial and scaled measurement simultaneously opens up the possibility of bringing together forms of sociological conceptualization and analysis which have for too long been pursued in isolation (Hope, 1972, pp. 123ff). Finally, permissible combinations of unit group and employment status (Table 6.5) should be referred to as occupation grading units, a term which we sometimes abbreviate to o.g.u.

TABLE 6.6

A collapsed version of the scale

Rank Order	Descriptive title (and occupations of greatest numerical importance)†	Constituent categories from complete scale	Average scale value (i.e. median of scale values of constituent categories)	% in Oxford Occupational Mobility Sample (Employed males age 20–64, resident in England & Wales, 1972. N = 9,457)	% in Employed Male Population of England & Wales aged 20–64. 1% Sample Census 1971. N = 121,547
1	Self-employed Professionals (Doctors; lawyers; accountants; dentists; surveyors; architects; pharmacists; engineers; stock and insurance brokers)	1701 2102 1702 0102 1703 2001 0903 0103	75	0·99	0·78
2	Salaried Professionals: higher grade (Engineers; accountants and company secretaries; surveyors; doctors; natural scientists; architects and town planners; university teachers; lawyers; airline pilots)	1906 1801 1802	71	5·27	4·78
3	Administrators and Officials: higher grade (Managers in large commercial enterprises and public utilities; sales managers; senior civil servants; local authority senior officers; also includes company directors, n.e.c.)	0601 0609 0602 0701 0603 4301 0607 0605	69	4·96	2·88**

4	Industrial Managers: large enterprises (Managers in engineering, extractive industries, general manufacturing and construction; personnel managers in all large establishments)	0606 0604	66	2·09	1·40
5	Administrators and Officials: lower grade (Police officers; radio and telegraph officers)	1402 2301 2201	65	1·04	0·88
6	Technicians: higher grade (Work study engineers; computer programmers; draughtsmen; laboratory technicians)	1903 2302	64	2·43	2·84
7	Large Proprietors (Working owners of large shops and service agencies)	0303 0403 0101 0402 0301 0201 0104 0302 0304 0401 0404 0501	63	0·35	0·02

Rank Order	Descriptive title (and occupations of greatest numerical importance)†	Constituent categories from complete scale	Average scale value (i.e. median of scale values of constituent categories)	% in Oxford Occupational Mobility Sample (Employed males age 20–64, resident in England & Wales, 1972. N = 9,457)	% in Employed Male Population of England & Wales aged 20–64. 1% Sample Census 1971. N = 121,547
8	Industrial and Business Managers: small enterprises (Managers in commerce, public utilities, engineering, extractive industries, general manufacturing and construction; personnel managers in all small establishments)	1404	62	0·87	2·41
9	Self-employed Professionals: lower grade (Parochial clergy; entertainers; artists; journalists)	1704 2101	62	0·35	0·33
10	Salaried Professionals: lower grade (Primary and secondary school teachers; civil service executive officers; social welfare workers; male nurses; public health inspectors; journalists; commercial artists)	1803 1904 1901	61	3·53	3·01
11	Farmers and Farm Managers	3901	58	0·86	0·79

12	Supervisors of Nonmanual Employees: higher grade (Supervisors of clerical employees)	2202	57	0·95	0·41
13	Small Proprietors (Working owners of small shops and service agencies; small builders; painters and decorators; hoteliers, boarding-house keepers and restaurateurs)	1002 1102 1202 0901 0902 1101 1001 1201 1103 3502 3401	57	3·73	2·75
14	Managers in Services and Small Administrative Units (Managers of shops and service agencies; office managers; hotel and restaurant managers)	0608 1406 1401 1902 1403 1407	53	2·04	3·02
15	Technicians: lower grade (Electrical and electronic engineers; Post Office technicians; auto-engineers; radio engineers; fire brigade men)	3102 3104 3105	51	3·88	3·69
16	Supervisors of Nonmanual Employees: lower grade (Supervisors of sales personnel)	2203	48	0·44	0·26

Rank Order	Descriptive title (and occupations of greatest numerical importance)†	Constituent categories from complete scale	Average scale value (i.e. median of scale values of constituent categories)	% in Oxford Occupational Mobility Sample (Employed males age 20–64, resident in England & Wales, 1972. N = 9,457)	%in Employed Male Population of England & Wales aged 20–64. 1% Sample Census 1971. N = 121,547
17	Supervisors of Manual Employees: higher grade (Foremen in engineering, construction, communications, and mining)	4401 1501 3002 3003 3001 3008 1601 3004 3007 0801	47	5·09	3·03**
18	Skilled Manual Workers in Manufacturing: higher grade (Maintenance and other fitters; millwrights; tool-makers; pattern-makers)	3106	46	5·20	5·89
19	Self-Employed Workers: higher grade (Shopkeepers; painters and decorators; carpenters and joiners; jobbing builders; publicans)	3402 3702 3601 3604 3701 3403 3603 1203 3602 1301	43	3·08	3·69
20	Supervisors of Manual Employees: lower grade (Foremen in warehousing, distribution, transport, chemicals,	3005 1405 3006 4101 1905	42	2·78	1·74

21	Nonmanual Employees in Administration and Commerce (Clerical workers; cashiers; commercial travellers)	2303	40	6·46	7·68
22	Skilled Manual Workers in Manufacturing: intermediate grade (Machine setters; sheetmetal workers; precision instrument makers; printers and compositors; glass and ceramic formers; also includes 'other ranks' in the Armed Services)	3101 3107 4501	38	3·88	3·55**
23	Skilled Manual Workers in Construction (Carpenters and joiners; painters and decorators; bricklayers)	3103	38	4·41	4·04
24	Smallholders without Employees	4001	37	0·73	0·72
25	Service Workers: higher grade (Cooks; stewards; hairdressers)	2501 2801 2601	37	0·48	0·50

Rank Order	Descriptive title (and occupations of greatest numerical importance)†	Constituent categories from complete scale	Average scale value (i.e. median of scale values of constituent categories)	% in Oxford Occupational Mobility Sample (Employed males age 20–64, resident in England & Wales, 1972. N = 9,457)	% in Employed Male Population of England & Wales aged 20–64. 1% Sample Census 1971. N = 121,547
26	Semi-Skilled Manual Workers in Manufacturing (Machine-tool operators; press operators; assemblers and routine inspectors; chemical process workers; food and other process workers)	3201	36	6·02	6·33
27	Skilled Manual Workers in Transport, Communications and Services, and Extractive Industries (Coalminers; operators of cranes and earth-moving equipment; engine drivers; steel erectors and riggers)	3108 3109 3110	36	2·77	2·84
28	Service Workers: intermediate grade (Shop salesmen and assistants)	2304 2402	35	0·93	1·39

No.	Occupation	Codes			
29	Self-Employed Workers: intermediate grade (Taxi drivers; carriers; café owners; entertainers)	3605 3606 3501 3801 4002	35	0·90	0·90
30	Skilled Manual Workers in Manufacturing: lower grade (Plant and engine operators; locksmiths, engravers and other metal working craftsmen; moulders, furnacemen and forgemen; sawyers and woodworkers; butchers; bakers)	3111	33	5·02	4·97
31	Agricultural Workers	4201	31	1·56	1·22
32	Semi-Skilled Manual Workers in Construction and Extractive Industries (Roofers, asphalters and cable layers; demolition workers; surface workers in mining and quarrying)	3203 3202	30	2·06	1·38

Rank Order	Descriptive title (and occupations of greatest numerical importance)†	Constituent categories from complete scale	Average scale value (i.e. median of scale values of constituent categories)	% in Oxford Occupational Mobility Sample (Employed males age 20–64, resident in England & Wales, 1972 N = 9,457)	% in Employed Male Population of England & Wales aged 20–64. 1% Sample Census 1971. N = 121,547
33	Semi-Skilled Manual Workers in Transport, Communications and Services (Lorry drivers; warehousemen; packers and labellers; storekeepers; postal workers; bus and coach drivers; roundsmen; ambulance men; deckhands; railway lengthmen; dock workers; gardeners and groundsmen; dry-cleaners and pressers)	3204 3301 3112	28	10·05	10·40
34	Service Workers; lower grade (Caretakers; doormen; guards and attendants; telephone operators; waiters; barmen and counter hands)	2401 2901	27	1·31	1·71
35	Unskilled Manual Workers (General labourers; factory labourers; building site labourers; railway porters; kitchen porters; office and industrial cleaners; messengers)	3302	18	3·12	6·11

36	Self-Employed Workers: lower grade (Street vendors; jobbing gardeners)	3703	18	0·31	0·23
				99·94	98·57**

† Based on data from the 1971 1 per cent Sample Census. To determine the full range of titles covered by a category it is necessary to work back from its reference number to its constituent OPCS unit groups (see p. 95 above). Note that the same occupation titles may be given for two or more categories, where these are associated with different employment statuses.

** Officers, NCOs and Other Ranks in the armed forces are assigned, respectively, to collapsed categories 3, 17, and 22. The Census makes no distinction among ranks and so the 1·49 per cent of the Sample Census who are in the armed services cannot be distributed among the three categories.

APPENDIX A

THE OXFORD INQUIRY

Proficiency in grading to the most rigid standards is easily acquired in practice, although a precise, and at the same time, simple definition of those standards in words or pictures is a matter of difficulty.

A spokesman of the Ministry of Agriculture
quoted by J. O. Urmson, 'On grading' (1950)

Purpose of the inquiry

In the study based on a sample of electors in the city of Oxford which is briefly reported in chapter 2, we were carrying out what amounts to an inquiry into the nature and validity of the process of occupation grading. This enquiry, however, must not be confused with a validation study, in the ordinary sense of that term. As we have explained in the Introduction to this volume, we draw a sharp distinction between the means by which a measuring instrument is produced and the subsequent investigation of its validity and reliability. We do not, in fact, suppose that one particular method of construction—for example the relatively technical and objective techniques that we have employed—will inevitably produce a more valid or more reliable scale than an alternative method—for example the subjective judgement of an experienced worker in the field of inquiry. We do not, that is, have any general belief in mode of construction as a guarantee of validity, though, provided that its approach is basically sound, one may suppose that a method which involves making empirical checks at each stage of the procedure will have advantages over an entirely *a priori* approach.

Once a measuring instrument has been produced, its validation involves ignoring the means by which it was produced, treating it as a set of given rules and procedures, applying those rules and procedures to the population of interest, and showing, by as independent a criterion as can be found, that the resulting scale values for a representative sample of individuals from the population deviate from the criterion values only because of error in either the criterion or the scale.*

* The minimum desideratum in this formulation of the problem of validation is that the systematic errors (biases) of the criterion and the scale be independent of one another. However, the presence of substantial systematic error in either leads to the unhappy situation of a validity coefficient (squared correlation between the scale and the criterion, after correction for attenuation due to random error in the latter) which is substantially lower than the reliability of the scale. This must lead the user of the scale to suspect that it may be measuring some factor or factors over and above the characteristic which it is supposed to measure, and in consequence that correlations between the scale and other variables may be in respect of these additional factors as well as, or rather than, in respect of the ostensible characteristic. These basic considerations of measurement theory are mentioned briefly here because sociologists have, in practice, been slow to subject their scales and instruments to the standard investigations which are demanded by the inherent logic of empirical research. We take the view that even the best quantitative social research will continue to produce only provisional conclusions until the measures of its main variables

In the Oxford inquiry we were carrying out not a validation study, but an investigation of what it is that people are capable of doing when they grade occupations. There is ample evidence that members of the public can grade occupations with a fair degree of inter-subjective agreement. Our problem was to try to tease out the substance and the structure of what they are agreeing about; that is, to apprehend the general nature of the characteristics which determine their view of the relative social standing of occupations, and to investigate possible ways in which they might structure those characteristics in arriving at a judgement. In analysing the data from this inquiry we examine a proposition put forward by Duncan and Artis and summarized by Duncan (1961) as follows:

It has been pointed out in previous work on the stratification of individuals in a community that there is no reason why judges of 'general standing' may not simultaneously agree on the ranking of subjects and disagree on the criteria of ranking, provided the several bases of ranking are interrelated. The analogous argument in regard to the ranking of occupations applies here.

The analysis is complex but this is inevitable in an area where we are trying to pick out one target among a fairly tightly clustered set of targets. Our defence for imposing these complexities on the reader may be summed up in an observation by Webb *et al.* (1966),

In the social sciences . . . we have no measuring devices as carefully compensated to control all irrelevancies as is the galvanometer. There simply are no social science devices designed with so perfect a knowledge of all the major relevant sources of variation . . . Our measures . . . tap multiple processes and sources of variance of which we are as yet unaware. At such a stage of development, the theoretical impurity and factorial complexity of every measure are not niceties for pedantic quibbling but are overwhelmingly and centrally relevant in all measurement applications which involve inference and generalization.

In pursuing our aims we were faced with a problem which is basic to all psychological research, and that is the problem of inferring the presence, in a complex and untidy real-life situation, of a function, capacity, or trait which has been demonstrated to exist only in an experimental situation which has been tightly controlled so as to exclude the possibility that other possible functions etc. are at work. In our inquiry the contrast is one only of degree, since the 'real-life' situation which we are trying to explain is the somewhat artificial task of grading occupations according to their 'social standing' and the 'experimental'

have been systematically validated. This is not to say that the sociologist should pursue high coefficients without regard to the theoretical or practical importance of the characteristic which he is trying to measure. Personality research has been trivialized by the use of highly reliable tests of functions which appear to have little psychological import. In much macro-sociological research employment of a measuring instrument with a low reliability may imply little more than the use of larger samples. Much more dangerous than a high degree of random error is the gap which so often yawns between the sum of the factor variances of an instrument (i.e. its reliability) and the extent to which it has been shown to measure a particular factor (its squared validity). This last point is expanded in the following section.

situation is the slightly more controlled task of grading occupations on possible elements of their social standing.

The model which we employ to represent the process which goes on in people's heads when they grade occupations on the single attribute of 'social standing' (as in the typical prestige-grading study) is that they have at least two criteria in mind and their judgement is a weighted average of their assessment of the positions of occupations on the criteria. The criteria are, we suppose, not incommensurable and can be regarded as axes of a space with at least two dimensions. Indeed, the model is essentially one which regards people's conceptions of occupations as a distribution of points in a Euclidean space of minimal dimensionality two. The positioning of axes in this space can be manipulated by the research worker. (We shall show, in fact, that when we impose a set of four axes on our graders, and then infer the structure of the relations among the axes from analysis of the distribution of occupation-points, there is a high degree of similarity between the average of the structures employed by one sample of graders and the average of another sample.) The space to which we allude is a postulate of our model. Without it, it is not possible to state some of the questions which we seek to answer. It is always possible that, when members of a sample are grading the social standing of occupations, some graders are operating in a unifactorial (i.e. one-dimensional) space (apart from error). However, what we have shown in the four-dimensional inquiry reported below is that graders *have the capacity* to work in a space of higher dimensionality, and that what they do in that space fits very well what they do in the ordinary single-attribute prestige-grading task. If we then make the assumption that they actually do in the single-attribute task what they have shown, in the multi-dimensional task, that they are capable of doing, it becomes possible to analyse the pattern of their gradings in the latter task in order to separate out its two basic structural features: namely, the extent of correlation among the perceived attributes, and the existence of cognitive consensus in the way in which the relevance of these attributes to occupational standing is viewed. These two aspects of structure are explained, illustrated, and elaborated below. In this brief introductory outline of the logic of our argument it is enough to say that we give reasons for supposing that both correlation and cognitive consensus exist, and that consensus is as strong between individuals in different social collectivities as between individuals within the same collectivity. Because the correlation whose degree we compute is correlation among axes imposed by the investigators, we cannot use it to estimate the correlation of such axes as are actually employed when none is imposed (though the extent of correlation among the imposed axes does show that people are capable of making quite clear subjective distinctions among attributes even when the attributes are factual characteristics of occupations which are objectively associated). Nevertheless, what we can assert is that it may not be necessary to explain the phenomena typically observed in prestige-grading inquiries simply by supposing a very high degree of correlation among the postulated component attributes of occupational standing (as they are subjectively conceived by members of the general public) since it is possible that there exists a substantial measure of agreement in the weighting schemes which are applied to axes which display only a moderate degree of correlation. The phenomena of prestige-gradings, therefore, are quite likely to be to some degree overdetermined in that they would not be significantly different if either correlation or consensus were less than it actually is.

Consensus and concurrence

The following sections describe a study which was designed to subject to empirical analysis our interpretation of the process by which occupations are graded and to provide estimates of the extent of various kinds of similarity among individuals in the way in which they carry out this process. The study was designed according to principles which were explored in a pilot inquiry (Goldthorpe and Hope, 1972) because these enable us not only to distinguish various types or aspects of agreement or consensus, but also, more fundamentally, to distinguish between consensus in the sense of agreement in the application of principles and mere concurrence which is the distorted empirical manifestation of such agreement.

In spite of its practical importance, the distinction between consensus and concurrence, or the parallel distinction between stability and reliability, is one which is greatly neglected by empirical research workers. Only too often the research worker who has not apprehended the importance of the examination of negative evidence is content with having established some degree of correlation between two measuring instruments, and he neglects to examine the sources of their failure to agree. Because this omission is so common in sociology it seems desirable to draw attention to its inherent dangers by means of a particularly simple illustrative example, which is based on practical experience in the psychological field, before embarking on a description of the complexities which occur when we seek to distinguish between error on the one hand, and dissensus or function instability on the other, in the field of occupation grading.*

*These introductory remarks will be easier to understand if the reader appreciates that in making them we are distinguishing four exclusive and exhaustive sections, proportions or components of the variance of the grading of a certain occupation by a certain grader on a certain occasion. The four components are: (a) the mean of an occupation's grades over many graders and many occasions of grading, (b) the deviation of a particular grader's assessment of an occupation from that of the average grader (dissensus), (c) the deviation of an occupation's grade on one occasion from its average grade over a temporal series of gradings (function instability), and (d) random error. Observed agreement or concurrence is ordinarily estimated by a correlation coefficient which is equivalent to the ratio $\frac{a+c}{a+b+c+d}$. The terms c and d are clearly irrelevant to the question of how much structured disagreement there is among grades and so we replace the preceding coefficient by the simple, direct ratio $\frac{a}{a+b}$ and refer to this as a measure of underlying agreement or consensus. Similarly we measure function stability by the simple ratio $\frac{a}{a+c}$.

In fact the empirical inquiry which we report below involves a more detailed partitioning of the variance of occupation gradings than the four-component model described here

Let us suppose that a psychological test has been validated by correlating it with some independent criterion measure which is known to be an unbiased measure of the function or characteristic which the test is supposed to measure. The correlation, which is an estimate of the validity of the test, is corrected for attenuation due to the unreliability of the criterion. The corrected validity coefficient is an estimate of the correlation of the test with a perfectly reliable criterion and its square tells us the proportion of the variance of the characteristic which is predictable from knowledge of test scores, and also the proportion of the variance of the test which is predictable from knowledge of persons' true positions on the characteristic. Thus if the corrected validity coefficient is 0·8 we may say that 64 per cent of the variance of the test is valid variance. Although this proportion might be interpreted as informing us that our test is reasonably valid, it does not of itself tell us how useful the test is likely to prove in practice, since we do not yet know the nature of the non-valid 36 per cent of the variance. The most basic information which we must have before using the test is its unreliability, that is, the extent to which the variance of the test may be attributed to random error. The simplest, and in many respects the most desirable, outcome of an investigation of the reliability of the test would be a reliability coefficient of 0·64 since, in this case, any correlation between the test and any other characteristic X may be attributed exclusively to an underlying correlation between the characteristic measured by the test and X. If, however, the reliability is high, let us say 0·90, then we are left with $90 - 64 = 26$ per cent of the variance of the test which is measuring characteristics which have yet to be determined, and the test may correlate, say, 0·5 with X solely with respect to these unknown characteristics, or with respect to some combination of its valid and its non-valid (but nevertheless reliable) variance.

It is hoped that this illustration, drawn from a field which is remote from our present concerns, will establish, in the minds of those who might balk at the complexities of our preparatory investigation of the process of occupational grading, the necessity for distinguishing between mere observed correlation or manifest concurrence and inferred degree of underlying agreement, over time or between persons. The analysis of the pilot inquiry (Goldthorpe and Hope, 1972) showed that, by making certain assumptions which appear to be reasonable and which are not contradicted by the evidence, it is possible to make a number of significant advances on the simple argument from observed concurrence to the presence of some degree of some type of consensus, which is the greatest degree of inferential precision that the conventional design of prestige rating experiments can afford.

We have been at pains to point out two weaknesses of the usual analysis and to provide techniques for estimating the relative importance of the components of a more adequate theoretical formulation. The first and very obvious weakness

---

since it is designed to allow us to investigate a further aspect of consensus and stability, namely consensus on, and stability of, the profile of an occupation over a set of attributes. Nevertheless the guiding principle of the analysis remains unchanged, namely that every coefficient should directly estimate the strength of one and only one effect. This is achieved by excluding irrelevant terms from its numerator and from its denominator.

is that the kind of average inter-grader agreement of 0·5 or so which emerges from a typical grading inquiry does not really indicate the extent of concurrence because it does not give us any information on the components of agreement or on the components of the failure to agree. In particular, it does not distinguish between error and positive disagreement. In our earlier paper we showed how this distinction could be made and we gave an example of the sort of research design which would allow agreement and the failure to agree to be disaggregated into theoretically meaningful components which are, in principle, independent and additive.

The second, and perhaps more subtle, error in the simple argument from concurrence to consensus may be illustrated by constructing a very simple model of what an informant is doing when he is assessing occupation titles. Let us suppose that a grader arrives at the 'social standing' of an occupation by a process of applying a vector of weights (some of which may be zero) to a set of axes. Let us also suppose, for the sake of simplicity, that these axes are objective characteristics of occupations such as their pay and educational requirements, so that there is a structure of correlation among the axes which is a 'given' and common to all informants. To simplify yet further, let us suppose that every informant has perfect knowledge of the true position of every occupation on every axis. (Unrealistic as they are, these suppositions are made simply to allow the point we wish to make to stand out as clearly as possible.) Then we may distinguish two possibilities: one in which the correlations among the axes are very high, say of the order of 0·9, and the other in which the correlations among the axes are moderate, say of the order of 0·5 or less. In the former case informants may bring very different sets of weights to the grading task and yet produce a high degree of concurrence; for example informant A may give a non-zero weight only to characteristic X and informant B may give a non-zero weight only to characteristic Y and yet the correlation between their gradings will be of the order of 0·9. But in the latter case—that of moderate or low correlations among axes—a high degree of concurrence will emerge only from the application of relatively similar vectors of weights.

In fact we do not have access to the correlation structure of the axes of the non-subjective space in which the social standing of occupations is assessed. But, in the Oxford inquiry which is reported below, we were able to offer informants a possible set of axes and to correlate their *conceptions* of the positions of occupations on these axes. We are able to show that this structure is, on average, quite remarkably constant from one social collectivity to another, and that this implies that, on average, the weighting system brought to bear on the assessment of occupations shows a high degree of consensus among collectivities. We also show that dissensus does exist to a significant if small degree, but that it appears to be personally rather than socially determined.

Design and conduct of the Oxford inquiry

Our preliminary thinking on the essential nature and empirical validity of the assessment of occupations by the general public was guided by the results of our

TABLE A1

The forty occupation titles graded by respondents

1. Actor
2. Agricultural labourer
3. Airline pilot
4. Ambulance man
5. Auctioneer and valuer
6. Bricklayer
7. Building site labourer
8. Bus driver
9. Business manager
10. Butcher (own shop)
11. Carpenter
12. Car worker
13. Civil engineer
14. Clergyman
15. Clerk
16. Coalminer
17. Crane operator
18. Doctor (general practitioner)
19. Farmer
20. Foreman (engineering factory)
21. Foundry worker
22. Ladies hairdresser
23. Nurse
24. Plumber
25. Policeman
26. Postman
27. Primary school teacher
28. Printer
29. Process worker (chemical industry)
30. Publican
31. Radar mechanic
32. Railway porter
33. Senior civil servant
34. Shoe repairer (own shop)
35. Shop assistant
36. Silversmith
37. Social worker
38. Solicitor
39. Textiles worker
40. Upholsterer

first small-scale grading studies. In order to test the views we had formed on the basis of this work, and also in order to make a more stringent test of the generally accepted view that assessment of occupations is highly stable from one social collectivity to another, and from one grading task to another, we designed an inquiry which involved drawing two random samples from the electoral register of the city of Oxford. The inquiry was carried out in 1971.

Members of one sample were given an occupation grading task of the conventional kind. The forty occupations listed in Table A1 were typed on individual pieces of card and respondents, who were interviewed by research assistants, were asked to place the cards in order of the *social standing* of the occupations, that is to grade them on the same characteristic as that used in the inquiry by Hall and Jones (1950). Sixty-nine of a sample of 88 completed the task, representing a response rate of 78 per cent. The titles in Table A1 were chosen to represent the range of the 26 Occupational Orders distinguished by the Office of Population Censuses and Surveys. In selecting titles we had regard to the number and variety of unit groups within each order (OPCS, 1970, pp. xxiii–xxxv) and to the need for the titles to be publicly recognizable.

Respondents in the second sample were asked, also by research assistants, to grade the same forty occupations, but their task was the more complex and unusual one which we devised in our pilot studies. A respondent was asked to grade the occupations first according to the *Standard of living* (S) of their typical incumbents, then according to their *Power and influence over other people* (I), then according to their *Level of qualifications* (Q), and finally according to their *Value to society* (V). We refer to this sample as the 'four-dimensional sample'. The four attributes, axes, or dimensions were selected (a) because they extend over the range of characteristics most often mentioned by respondents in conventional occupation prestige studies when they are asked what attributes of occupations determined their judgement (Taft 1953; Tiryakian 1958; Reiss 1961); and (b) because in our preliminary empirical work we had found that these characteristics could be assessed with roughly equal accuracy by respondents.* The respondents to the four-dimensional inquiry were approached on a second occasion between two and three months after their initial performance of the task and they were asked to repeat it exactly as on the first occasion. 176 (50 per cent) of the 348 members of the sample completed the task on both occasions and a further 42 (13 per cent) completed it on the first occasion only. Of the remaining 130 persons 53 were not contacted, mainly because they had moved or died, 30 were too old, ill or disabled to perform the task successfully (there was no upper age limit to the population) 5 were lost for miscellaneous reasons, and 42 refused to grant an interview.

---

* In one of the pilot studies the attribute 'the interest of the work' was found to have a higher error component than its companions and this discrepancy threw some doubt on the estimates of various terms in the analysis. We surmised that the interest of a job is difficult to assess both because the respondent (and this is especially true of women who are not economically active) may be uncertain about the nature of the work, and because he or she may have difficulty in assessing the probable subjective attitude of those who hold the job.

In the four-dimensional inquiry refusals on either the first or the second occasion accounted for four-fifths of total non-response. The response rate cannot be regarded as satisfactory. However, the analyses do tend to suggest that, in an occupation grading study, the effect of sample attrition by refusal to participate introduces no bias into the results but merely serves to reduce error by omitting potential informants who are in fact less aware of the nature and standing of occupations or less willing to take pains in the performance of the task. This supposition arises partly from the finding, reported below, that membership of a particular social collectivity makes no apparent difference to gradings, and it is difficult to imagine why the collectivity 'non-respondent' should be an exception to this general finding. It also arises from a comparison between those who completed the four-dimensional task on both occasions and those who completed it once but refused to participate on a second occasion. The only difference which emerges from analyses of the data for these two categories of respondent is that the latter have a considerably larger error term than the former and a correspondingly reduced component of variance for the general factor of 'Occupations'.

In performing the grading task, respondents in both samples were permitted to set about the sorting of the cards bearing the names of occupations in any manner they pleased. They were asked to rank the occupations by placing the cards in a column, and they were allowed to give two or more occupations an equal rank by placing their cards side by side. The sample grading in terms of 'social standing' performed one such ranking and the four-dimensional sample provided four rankings on each of two occasions.

The occupation or occupations in the top rank of a column were given a score of one, those in the second rank were given a score of two, and so on down to the occupations in the lowest rank, for which the score was the number of discrete ranks distinguished by the respondent. The scores of the forty occupations within a column were centred about their mean and standardized so that every column of forty scores has a mean of zero and a variance of one. The reasoning underlying this scoring procedure is described in the earlier paper (Goldthorpe and Hope, 1972, p. 45). The detailed analysis of the four-dimensional study also followed the pattern of the analyses reported in that paper. Seven respondents were omitted from the analysis of the four-dimensional sample because they did not provide complete data and a further nine were omitted because they graded all occupations as equal in at least one of their eight columns of rankings.

Empirical findings

The evidence of the Oxford study, in so far as it is relevant to our main purpose of constructing a grading scale for all male occupations on the basis of popular assessments, leads to the following conclusions.

1. The stability, over a period of two or three months, with which the general public grades occupations is high for an individual respondent and very high for the mean of a moderately large sample of respondents.

TABLE A2

Analysis of variance of centred and standardized gradings of forty occupations on four dimensions by 160 respondents on two occasions. All effects are assumed to be random.

Source	d.f.	Sum of squares	Mean square	Variance component
Occupations	39	22,880·1273	586·6699	0·4236
Occupations × Respondents	6,201	7,237·0815	1·1671	0·0811
Occupations × Occasions	39	16·1168	0·4133	−0·0002
Occupations × Dimensions	117	5,122·8413	43·7850	0·1349
Occupations × Respondents × Occasions	6,201	2,146·2730	0·3461	0·0242
Occupations × Respondents × Dimensions	18,603	7,831·7673	0·4210	0·0859
Occupations × Occasions × Dimensions	117	50·2901	0·4298	0·0011
Error	18,603	4,635·5027	0·2492	0·2492
Sum	49,920	49,920·0000	—	0·9998

Table A2 contains an analysis of variance of the centred and standardized gradings by the four-dimensional sample. The process of centring each column of gradings about its mean has eliminated the main terms for Respondents (d.f. = 159) Occasions (d.f. = 1), and Dimensions (d.f. = 3) as well as all interactions which do not include Occupations. The standardization of each column to unit variance has constrained the total sum of squares to equal the total degrees of freedom. In the computation of variance components all four terms of the design are assumed to be random. (In the earlier paper 'Dimensions' was assumed to be a fixed effect, but further consideration of its nature persuaded us that in sampling respondents one is implicitly introducing a sampling distribution for Dimensions, because each person has a somewhat idiosyncratic idea of the nature of a particular dimension, and this means that differences among respondents are not simply due to disagreement about the position of occupations on identical dimensions, but also represent some degree of disagreement on the nature of the dimensions. This in turn means that the variance of the level of an occupation, averaged across all four dimensions for a particular respondent, contains a random component contributed by the covariance structure for that respondent.) When a completely random model is assumed, and when each column of gradings has been centred and standardized, the sum of the variance components is necessarily one, apart from rounding errors.

The analysis shows that 0·2492 or 25 per cent of the variance of gradings derive from the 'interaction' of all four terms and we repeat our earlier practice of assuming that this variance is entirely attributable to random error; it is as such that it features in the equations from which the estimates of variance are derived.

The variance component for Occupations × Respondents × Occasions, although perhaps not negligible, is quite small. It indicates that there may be some tendency for the individual respondent to change his mind on the relative over-all standing of occupations from occasion to occasion, but the degree of change accounts for only 2 per cent of the total variance. However, bearing in mind the distinction which we have drawn between observed concurrence and underlying consensus which, in its present application, is a distinction between the computed self-correlation of individual respondents and their estimated extent of agreement with themselves over time, uncontaminated by error, we may calculate the latter from the Occupations × Respondents and the Occupations × Respondents × Occasions terms of the analysis as follows:

$$\frac{0·0811}{0·0811 + 0·0242} = 0·7700 \, .$$

It should be emphasized that this coefficient, for which we coined the name *coefficient of personal-general stability* measures the stability of the deviation of an individual's assessment of occupations from the assessment by the sample as a whole, irrespective of the relative importance of such deviations in the total variance. It shows that, although these idiosyncratic judgements account for only 0·0811 or 8 per cent of the total variance, they are nevertheless remarkably stable over time.

The two components Occupations × Occasions and Occupations × Occasions × Dimensions are both so close to zero as to be entirely negligible, thus indicating that, whatever the individual respondent may do, a mean taken over the sample of individuals show no tendency (a) to manifest change in the relative positions of occupations on the central dimension, which is the average of the four particular dimensions; or (b) to show any more complicated shifts in the positioning of occupations in which stability on the central dimension might be the result of a series of self-compensating movements on the particular dimensions. The coefficients which appropriately represent these two aspects of stability are Mahmoud's (1955) *coefficient of person stability*

$$\frac{0\cdot4236}{0\cdot4236 + (-0\cdot0002)} = 1\cdot0004$$

and Hope's (1969) *coefficient of pattern or profile stability*

$$\frac{0\cdot1349}{0\cdot1349 + 0\cdot0011} = 0\cdot9917 \ .$$

The former is the stability with which the sample locates occupations on the mean or centroid of the four dimensions or attributes. In this context it may be termed a *coefficient of common-general stability*; that is, a measure of the stability of the variance which is *common* to respondents and *general* among dimensions. The latter is the stability of the pattern or profile of an occupation across the four dimensions, averaged over the sample as a whole, it may therefore be termed a *coefficient of common profile stability*.

There is, therefore, every reason to suppose that a sample of the general public can yield an assessment of the standing of occupations which will display no short-term fluctuation at all. In the short term, although the individual manifests some non-random alteration in his assessment of the over-all standing of occupations,* this averages out over individuals.

2. The four attributes or dimensions are not treated as synonymous, and the distinctions made among them are to some extent shared by respondents.

The extent of the shared discrimination among the attributes is indicated by the Occupations × Dimensions term which accounts for 0·1349 or 13 per cent of the total variance. The extent of the tendency of individuals to draw distinctions among the attributes which are deviations form the common pattern of distinctions is indicated by the Occupations × Respondents × Dimensions term which accounts for 0·0859 or 9 per cent of the total variance. The coefficient of pattern stability quoted above shows that the common distinctions, that is, the pattern of correlations among the axes averaged over the sample as a whole, are practically perfectly stable. The ascription of all the third-order interaction variance to error prevents us from computing a comparable coefficient for the individual deviations from the common pattern.

* This may of course simply be a learning process. One might find a greater degree of stability between a second and a third performance of the grading task.

In the earlier paper the device of a pooling square was employed to show how the variance components may be translated into estimates of 'true' correlation, that is, into measures of underlying agreement or association from which error and bias have been eliminated. Each of these estimates is an additive combination of variance components divided by the overall total which, for the completely random model, is one. They are reported in Table A3. The subscript r indicates an aspect of association measured within the gradings of a particular respondent. For example, the coefficient r_r is derived from the sum of the variance components for Occupations and Occupations $\times$ Respondents as

$$r_r = 0{\cdot}4236 + 0{\cdot}0811 = 0{\cdot}50$$

and represents the mean correlation between gradings of different attributes by the same respondent.* The element $0{\cdot}0811$ may be regarded as a halo effect, or tendency, within the gradings of a particular respondent, for occupations to deviate from the general norm in the same direction and to the same extent over all attributes. The subscript o similarly indicates association within a single occasion, and d indicates association within a particular dimension. Absence of a subscript indicates association across *different* respondents, occasions, or dimensions.

TABLE A3

Elements of the pooling square derived from the variance components of Table A2

r	$0{\cdot}4236$
r_r	$0{\cdot}5048$
r_o	$0{\cdot}4235$
r_d	$0{\cdot}5586$
r_{ro}	$0{\cdot}5288$
r_{rd}	$0{\cdot}7256$
r_{od}	$0{\cdot}5595$
r_{rod}	$1{\cdot}0000$

It was shown in the earlier paper (Goldthorpe and Hope, 1972, p. 74) that the appropriate estimate of overall reliability is the coefficient r_{rd} which is the average extent to which a respondent concurs with himself in grading occupations on a particular attribute at two points in time. In the present inquiry $r_{rd} = 0{\cdot}73$. Correcting r_r for attenuation due to unreliability by dividing it by r_{rd} gives a value of $0{\cdot}70$ as the average degree of splaying of the four attributes in the cognitive space of the individual respondent. The same correction applied to the Occupations $\times$ Dimensions term and to the Occupations $\times$ Respondents $\times$

---

* To which should be appended 'on different occasions'. r_{ro}, which is the correlation between attributes graded by the same respondent on the same occasion, is $0{\cdot}53$.

Dimensions term yields coefficients of 0·19 and 0·12. These three estimates necessarily sum to one, apart from rounding errors.

If the four attributes are assessed by four different respondents* the average extent of underlying agreement among the four is $r/r_{rd} = 0.58$.

TABLE A4

Correlations among the dimensions on which occupations were graded, and their correlations with the grand means over all 160 respondents, both occasions, and all four dimensions

		S	I	Q	V
Standard of Living	(S)	1·0000			
Power and influence	(I)	0·7275	1·0000		
Qualifications	(Q)	0·8602	0·8693	1·0000	
Value to society	(V)	0·4687	0·8527	0·7510	1·0000
Grand mean		0·8545	0·9517	0·9665	0·8404

The gradings of occupations on each dimension were averaged over all respondents and both occasions and the correlations among the four vectors of means are reported in Table A4. The mean of the six correlations between different dimensions is 0·75.

The upshot of this analysis is that, on average, two attributes share 70 per cent of their variance and are distinct to the extent of 30 per cent. The 30 per cent (which represents deliberate distinctions drawn among attributes and contains no component of error) splits into 19 per cent which is consensual and 12 per cent which represents dissensus in the sense of non-universal (but not necessarily entirely individual) discrimination among attributes which differs in some respect from the average pattern of discrimination.

3. Analysis by social collectivities within the sample confirms the over-all analysis and indicates some minor difference between collectivities.

Three different breakdowns of the sample were investigated—the two sexes, three age categories, and four occupation categories—and the analysis of Table A2 was repreated for each of the nine subdivisions. The analysis in terms of respondent's occupation is of the most general interest since it is the one which appeared most likely to reveal differences and dissensus between collectivities. For the

---

* Strictly speaking we should qualify this protasis by adding that the gradings on a particular attribute should have been obtained in a context of gradings on the other three attributes, the four being administered in the standard order of the present inquiry.

A further qualification which should be made to all references to the 'cognitive space' of respondents is that the measures of agreement refer to a certain distribution of occupations which is implicit in the selection of titles which respondents were given to grade. The list of titles may, for example, over-represent the higher-level occupations and under-represent the lower, but the measures of association do not include any weighting factor to correct for differential frequency. There is a sense, however, in which our list, which is a sample of distinct and relatively salient occupational roles, is probably more representative of the manifold of the cognitive space of individuals than a statistically purer random sample of occupation titles weighted by their frequency of occurrence.

purpose of this analysis each of the 160 respondents was assigned to one of the
following *ad hoc* categories:

A(n = 39)   Owners and proprietors of businesses and employees
              Professional and higher-level technical employees
              Administrators
              Managers (other than as in B)
              Officers in the Armed Services

B(n = 24)   Owners and proprietors of businesses without employees, freelance
                 workers (other than professionals or those in C)
              Supervisors, inspectors, and foremen (except in agriculture)
              Managers in small workshops, etc.
              Minor officials
              Clerical and sales workers
              Lower-level technicians and highly-skilled craftsmen
              N.C.O.s in armed services

C(n = 67)   Self-employed workers with minimal capital and skill
              Manual workers in manufacturing industry, construction, transport,
                 and mining
              Rank-and-file workers in services
              Agricultural workers (including foremen)
              Other ranks in armed services

D(n = 30)   Students*

The variance components (equivalent to the last column of Table A2, which is
reproduced) for the various terms of each analysis are reported in Table A5. It can
be seen that, as we move down the social scale from A to C, there is an increase
in the amount of error and a compensating decrease in the over-all amount of
agreement in the grading of occupations (the sum of the terms for Error and
Occupations is a constant). All the Occupations X Occasions and Occupations X
Occasions X Dimensions terms are very small so that both the common-general
stabilities and the common profile stabilities are very high (Table A6). The remaining terms in Table A5 are pretty uniform across the three categories and the
personal-general stabilities are roughly comparable (Table A6). Gradings by
students contain a lower proportion of error and a considerably higher degree of
discrimination among the dimensions than gradings by the other three collectivities
In consequence they have a higher coefficient of personal-general stability (Table A

4. The extent of consensus among social collectivities in the assessment of the
positions of occupations on the individual dimensions is very high indeed, so that
the pattern of splaying of the four axes is very similar from one collectivity to
another.

* By the date of this inquiry many students had succeeded in having their names placed on
  the Oxford electoral register.

TABLE A5

Components of variance in analyses of gradings of occupations on four dimensions by respondents classified by occupation (A, B, C, and Students) and by all respondents (cf. Table A2)

Source	A	B	C	Students	All
Categories of respondents n	39	24	67	30	160
Occupations	0·48	0·41	0·39	0·47	0·42
Occupations × Respondents	0·08	0·08	0·08	0·06	0·08
Occupations × Occasions	−0·00	−0·00	−0·00	0·00	−0·00
Occupations × Dimensions	0·13	0·11	0·12	0·21	0·13
Occupations × Respondents × Dimensions	0·02	0·03	0·03	0·01	0·02
Occupations × Respondents × Occasions	0·08	0·09	0·07	0·10	0·09
Occupations × Occasions × Dimensions	0·00	0·00	0·00	−0·00	0·00
Error	0·21	0·28	0·30	0·16	0·25
Sum	1·00	1·00	0·99	1·01	0·99

TABLE A6

Stability coefficients derived from the variance components of Table A5

Categories of respondents	A	B	C	Students	All
n	39	24	67	30	160
Common-general stability	1·00	1·00	1·00	1·00	1·00
Common profile stability	0·98	0·99	0·98	1·00	0·99
Personal-general stability	0·83	0·71	0·71	0·91	0·77

Within each of the four occupation categories of respondent the mean grading of an occupation was calculated over all respondents in the category for each of the two occasions. In this way eight forty-item vectors of means were obtained for a category, each representing one of the dimensions S, I, Q, and V on one occasion of grading. All the vectors were standardized and entered into an analysis of variance in which occupational categories of respondents took the place of the Respondents term in the previous analyses.

Adding together the Occupations and the Occupations × Dimensions terms in Table A7 we see that all but 3½ per cent of the variance of the mean gradings is accounted for it we simply assume that every collectivity has the same pattern of relations among the four attributes. This very high degree of consensus is graphically displayed in the spherical co-ordinate plot of Figure 1 (p. 17) in which the sixteen vectors of means (each being an average of vectors for the two occasions) are projected on to the surface of a sphere whose orthogonal axes are their first three principal components. (The first principal component lies in the centre of the plot and accounts for 80 per cent of the variance of the sixteen vectors. In all 97 per cent of the variance is retained in the three-dimensional plot of Figure 1. The point O is explained below). The lowest correlation between any two members of any set of four points is 0·940 (in the space as a whole, not merely in the three-dimensional space of the figure).

When the effect of unreliability is taken into account in order to arrive at an estimate of the various types of consensus and dissensus *within* collectivities it can be seen (Table A8) that the occupation categories A, B, and C are remarkably uniform while the students display a pattern of lower (common and personal) general variance which is offset by a higher degree of shared discrimination among the four attributes.

Putting together the analyses of Tables A7 and A8, we may infer that, although students operate with a more highly differentiated cognitive map of occupations than other collectivities, there is no difference worthy of note in the patterns of the weights which the average members of the collectivities bring to the grading task. The contrasts made by the students among the various aspects of occupationa standing are somewhat more extreme but they are nevertheless the same contrasts as those made by other collectivities.

TABLE A7

Analysis of variance in which the data are vectors of mean gradings of forty occupations on four dimensions by each of four categories of respondent. Respondents are classified in terms of their own occupational level and they performed the grading task on two occasions

Source	d.f.	Sum of squares	Mean square	Variance component
Occupations	39	989·2996	25·3667	0·7305
Occupations × Categories	117	12·7232	0·1087	0·0091
Occupations × Occasions	39	0·6659	0·0171	0·0000
Occupations × Dimensions	117	224·3858	1·9178	0·2351
Occupations × Categories × Occasions	117	1·7551	0·0150	0·0002
Occupations × Categories × Dimensions	351	12·4316	0·0354	0·0107
Occupations × Occasions × Dimensions	117	1·7990	0·0154	0·0003
Error	351	4·9397	0·0141	0·0141
Sum	1248	1248·0000	—	1·0000

TABLE A8

Proportions of true variance indicating the extent to which dimensions are splayed in the cognitive space of respondents classified by occupational level

Categories of respondents	A	B	C	Students	All
n	39	24	67	30	160
Variance which is general among the four dimensions	0·72	0·71	0·71	0·63	0·70
Consensual discrimination among dimensions	0·18	0·17	0·18	0·25	0·19
Dissensus in discrimination among dimensions	0·10	0·12	0·11	0·12	0·12
	1·00	1·00	1·00	1·00	1·01

5. The common-general factor of the gradings of occupations on our four dimensions is virtually identical with the one dimension employed in the conventional prestige-grading inquiry.

It will be recalled that another random sample of the Oxford electorate was asked to grade the same occupations, on one occasion only, on the single attribute 'social standing'. Four of the 69 respondents who completed the task were omitted from the analysis, two because their data were incomplete, and two because they ascribed the same social standing to all occupations. The mean correlation between pairs of respondents was 0·46.* The vector of mean gradings of the 65 members of the one-dimensional sample correlates 0·977 with the first principal component of the 16 mean vectors of the four-dimensional sample. Its projection in the space of Figure 1 (p. 17) is at point O. Its correlations with the remaining 15 components are in consequence all small, and the coefficient of determination, $R^2 = 0·986$, for its regression on the 16 SIQV vectors therefore exceeds $0·977^2 = 0·955$ by only 0·031. Lest it should be supposed that introducing the four collectivities severally into the analysis inflates these correlations, it should be said that the correlation[†] of the mean of the one-dimensional sample with the first principal component of S, I, Q, and V, where each of these is averaged over the four-dimensional sample as a whole, is 0·979 and R^2 is 0·970. If we substitute for the principal components a simple average across all 160 respondents, all four dimensions, and both occasions the correlation of the resulting forty-element vector of mean gradings by the four-dimensional sample with the mean vector of the one-dimensional sample is 0·978. It may therefore be concluded that not more than 5 per cent of the variance of a typical prestige grading task is unaccounted for by a simple average of the four attributes S, I, Q, and V. Any attempt to partition this 4 or 5 per cent among (a) error, (b) variance related to some combination of the dimensions, and (c) variance lying outside the space of the dimensions, would make demands which could not be met by any typical data of social research.

Summary of findings relevant to the construction of an occupation scale

The literature describing occupation grading studies contains ample evidence that respondents can grade occupations with some degree of agreement with one another, and some degree of covariance on different verbal formulations of the grading task. Once these facts have been firmly established, the important questions of estimation concern the extent of self-inconsistency and of instability over time, the extent of dissensus, and the degree to which verbally distinct

* The sample was broken down by occupation category of respondent into nonmanual (n = 27), manual (n = 26) and students (n = 11). One respondent could not be classified. The lowest correlation among the three mean vectors of grading of these collectivities was 0·87, which is the correlation between students and respondents in the manual category. In the absence of an estimate of error, it is not possible to estimate the extent of consensus underlying this degree of concurrence.

† It should perhaps be pointed out that a correlation between a principal component of one sample and a dimension derived from another sample differs from a latent root or a coefficient of multiple determination in that it is not subject to any algebraic constraint which tends to inflate its value.

attributes of occupations are denotatively distinguished by respondents. The inquiry reported here addressed itself to these questions and the analyses were designed, not primarily to demonstrate a positive degree of consensus or stability, but to find out whether dissensus and instability are either negligible in quantity or are such as to be eliminable by averaging over a modest number of respondents.

To put the point crudely: once some degree of concurrence has been established, the crucial problem becomes that of assessing the gap between the underlying degree of true association and perfect association. This is never an easy matter in the presence of substantial measurement error. Ways must be found of isolating possible error components and these involve the specification of models. One can never be positively sure that the models are appropriate, though they are open to falsification by the occurence of nonsensical estimates, such as negative variances. No such falsifying evidence has occurred in the analyses of this study.

One way of increasing confidence in a model is to over-complicate it in such a way that one and the same quantity is estimated by several routes. The basic analysis of variance model has passed this test, returning components which are vanishingly small for terms which, if our assumptions (derived from the analyses reported in the preliminary paper) are correct, represent a certain quantity subtracted from itself. A second positive way of testing the acceptability of a model is to apply it to different samples, and this we have successfully done in the analyses of sub-samples of respondents classified by occupation. The generally adequate performance of the models encourages us to believe that they may be regarded as satisfactory means for testing the unimportance of the gap between underlying consensus or stability and perfect agreement or invariableness—a matter which requires a good deal more precision than the mere establishing of some degree of positive correlation.

The Oxford inquiry has demonstrated that the gap between the attribute assessed in the conventional one-dimensional prestige-grading study and the centroid of a set of four attributes graded by an independent sample of respondents is, to some unknown extent, less than 5 per cent in terms of shared variance. We infer, therefore, that we are justified in using the findings of the four-dimensional study to interpret existing occupation prestige studies.

The four-dimensional inquiry shows that the general public can distinguish various aspects of the social standing of occupations, that the shared pattern of such distinctions is uniform among various occupational collectivities, and that the contrasts of light and shade in the pattern are also uniform except among students, for whom the same contrasts are somewhat sharper. Within any occupational collectivity there is, to a very similar degree, a pattern of personal (though not necessarily unshared, since sub-samples within the collectivity may deviate in the same respects) deviation from the collective mean pattern.

Measures of stability over a period of a few weeks demonstrate a uniform and very high degree of profile stability across the four attributes and a virtually perfect stability of the over-all mean position of occupations on the centroid which approximates closely to the ordinary prestige-grading dimension. From this it may be inferred that a grading scale derived from popular assessments of the standing of occupations will not decay rapidly after the date of its construction,* though only repeated assays at fairly wide intervals could adequately assess its current condition.

Although individual respondents display consistent differences from the mean over-all assessments of occupations, and the stability of these differences is not perfect, the extent of agreement among individuals indicates that a good approximation to the 'social standing' of an occupation may be obtained by averaging over a quite small random sample of graders. The nature of the distribution of these graders among collectivities is a matter of little moment.

The most salient findings of the Oxford inquiry are succinctly summarized in Figure 1, p. 17.

Summary of findings relevant to the interpretation of an occupation scale

The preceding section has summarized estimates of effects, each of which is defined by its status as a component of a model. The estimates are all quite reasonable and interpretable and they form a coherent set which, provided that we take the highest-order interaction term as specifying random error, exhausts a universe of possible effects.

In this section we turn to a discussion of the model itself and of the logical standing of the different kinds of assertion that we have made in employing it. In particular, we take up the question, posed in the first section of this appendix, of the two aspects of the structure of our assumed model: the correlation among attributes of occupations as these are conceived by graders, and the extent to which graders manifest cognitive consensus by applying similar weights to similarly-related attributes in arriving at a judgement of the relative social standing of occupations.

In order to simplify the discussion let us suppose that we have two attributes of occupations, X and Y, each of which is cognized by everyone in exactly the same way. The correlation between them, as cognized, is r. Suppose now that respondents A_1, A_2, and A_3, whose gradings of the 'social standing' of occupations lie entirely in the space of X and Y, display a certain pattern of correlations with the attributes. For the sake of simplifying the algebra we shall take all the correlations between graders and attributes to be simple functions of r:

	A_1	A_2	A_3
X	r	1·0	r
Y	$2r^2-1$	r	1·0

Then the regression coefficients for predicting (in each case with perfect accuracy) the occupation gradings of the three respondents are:

---

* Unless of course there is an increase in the rate of change of the flux of occupations on objective attributes.

	A_1	A_2	A_3
X	2r	1·0	0
Y	−1·0	0	1·0

let us suppose that the intercorrelations are:

	A_1	A_2	A_3
A_1		0·7	0
A_2			0·7
A_3			

with a consensus of 0·47.

The situation may be completely and simply represented by a vector diagram in two dimensions,

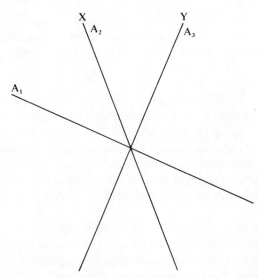

Now let us suppose that the gradings of three other respondents, B_1 B_2 and B_3 lie symmetrically arranged with respect to attribute Y just as do the gradings of A_1, A_2, and A_3 with respect to attribute X. Then it is obvious that the B's will reveal the same degree of consensus as the A's, namely 0·47, and that the mean B (actually represented by B_2) will correlate with the mean $A(A_2)$ to the degree that Y correlates with X. This is a situation in which we have a degree of within-collectivity consensus (0·47) but the correlation between the means of collectiviti (0·7) is wholly explicable in terms of the extent of correlation between the attributes; i.e. there is no reason to specify the presence of inter-collectivity consensus, even though members of the two collectivities overlap (the average correlation between an A and a B is 0·35).

By contrast, let us suppose that the A's rotate clockwise (through $22\frac{1}{2}°$ in the numerical example) until A_2 is half-way between X and Y and the B's similarly rotate anticlockwise until B_2 is also halfway between X and Y.

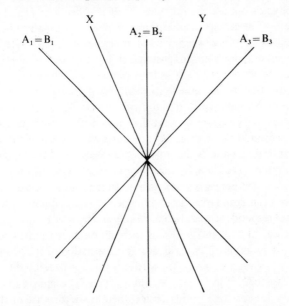

The extent of consensus within collectivities remains unchanged but the concurrence between the means of collectivities is now perfect. Knowing that a respondent belongs to a particular collectivity adds nothing to our knowledge of the way in which he 'operates the model'. The correlation between any two individuals tends to the same value irrespective of whether they both belong to the same collectivity.* Consensus exists within the superordinate collectivity consisting of both A's and B's to exactly the same extent as it does within each of these collectivities separately. Our next task therefore is to set out the argument for the probable existence of consensus within collectivities.

How do our artificial examples relate to what actually happens when respondents grade occupations on a single attribute of 'social standing'? We have some direct evidence from our main occupation grading inquiry in that 62 respondents graded the social standing of twenty occupations on two occasions. These are directly comparable with the respondents in the four-dimensional inquiry since both samples represent people who were willing to co-operate on two occasions.†
The degree of inter-respondent agreement (average correlation between two

* Actually the numerical example obscures this point since, by equating each A with a B, the over-all amount of agreement has been artificially inflated. This is analogous to ignoring the fact that the means of two samples from the same population will tend to differ by reason of sampling error.
† As noted above (p. 152) the evidence of the Oxford study is that there is a clear tendency for those who co-operate on two occasions to give more reliable gradings than those who co-operate on only one occasion.

respondents corrected for attenuation due to unreliability) is 0·72 over the sample as a whole. All our evidence leads us to believe that this will also be the extent of inter-respondent agreement within collectivities. Thus the extent to which individuals spread or splay out around the mean of their collectivity is a good deal smaller than the 0·47 of our artificial example. Indeed, 0·72 slightly exceeds the degree of association (0·70) between pairs of attributes with which respondents were asked to operate in the four-dimensional study, even though this figure is inflated by a halo effect of 0·12 (0·70 is the mean association among attributes all of which are assessed by the same individual; the mean degree of association between attributes assessed by different individuals is 0·58).

We are therefore in a position to assert that if, in grading the 'social standing' of occupations, respondents are typically operating with a set of attributes which has the same sort of dispersion as the set which they are capable of operating with when it is presented to them by the experimenters, then, within a collectivity, the extent of association between gradings by different individuals cannot be due simply to the extent of correlation among the perceived attributes. It would not be possible, if one respondent was grading wholly in terms of attribute X (i.e. giving a unit regression weight to X and zero weights to all other attributes), and another was grading wholly in terms of Y, for an average association of 0·72 to be achieved unless the average correlation among the attributes, as cognized by different individuals, was at least 0·72. If in fact the attributes typically employed in assessing social standing do not correlate to this degree, then the occurrence of this amount of inter-respondent association implies a degree of consensus in the sense that the weights for the regression of social standing on the attributes will all tend to be positive.

We are not, of course, in a position to say what attributes or combinations of attributes are employed with what relative frequencies when respondents grade on the central dimension which we interpret as the general desirability of occupations. We do not, however, need to assume that the typical extent of association among the attributes (as cognized by different individuals) is of the order of 0·7 or greater, since we have shown, in the four-dimensional study, that, when supplied with a set of attributes having a much looser degree of association than this, respondents are capable of achieving a substantial level of inter-respondent agreement.*

Thus high levels of inter-individual agreement are consistent with the occurrence of relatively low correlations among criteria of assessment. Indeed, as a consequence of the analysis of the four-dimensional study, we are in a better

* In fact the mean agreement between two respondents in the four-dimensional study is 0·82. This coefficient, which has been variously called an intraclass correlation (Burt, 1955), a coefficient of external consistency or equivalence (Mahmoud, 1955), and a coefficient of stability (Pilliner, 1965) is computed from the components of Table A2 as

$$\frac{4(0·4236) + 0·1349}{4(0·4236 + 0·0811) + 0·1349 + 0·0859}.$$

It represents the underlying consensus (observed concurrence corrected for unreliability) over the whole 'hand' of attributes.

position to assert the existence of consensus or shared weightings in the application of grading criteria to occupations than we are to make suppositions about the actual degree of correlation among attributes typically employed in the performance of the conventional prestige-grading task, as these are cognized, since we can only speculate as to what the latter are.

In an important sense it is never possible to analyse any complex psychological process into its constituents because it is always possible that the process suffers modification by the experimental procedures which are applied to the analysis. We can never know what complex of attributes respondents are using when they are actually reporting on only a single attribute. We cannot therefore test any assumptions which we might wish to make about the relations among those attributes. This, so far from justifying us in making any assumption we choose, such as that the attributes, as cognized, are highly correlated, should caution us to see what might be the case if our preferred assumption was in fact untrue. The four-dimensional study, by showing that respondents are capable of discriminating attributes quite markedly, and that they can display a high degree of consensus in the weighting of attributes, gives us a second line of attack on the problem of why people tend to agree in their assessment of occupations. We do not have to choose between the two elements of the explanation, or even to hazard a guess as to the balance between the two. In fact if both are at work to a marked degree the extent of over-all agreement is over-determined and one cannot sensibly ascribe the joint effect of the elements to either alone.

THE LONDON INQUIRY

In order to achieve commensurability in respondents' rankings of different subsets of representative occupation titles, we designed the grading task for our main inquiry so that every respondent began by grading a common set of 20 standard occupation titles. After he had assured the interviewer that he was quite happy with the ordering of the standard occupations, the respondent was then given a further set of 20 cards, each bearing the title of one of the 860 representative occupations, and he was asked to insert each of these into the ranking of the standard occupations at the point at which, in terms of its 'social standing', he believed it belonged. Respondents were informed that they could tie one or more representative occupation titles with a standard occupation title (or with several titles, if these had been tied in the preliminary grading) by placing them along-side the standard title; that they could place one or more ranks (i.e. single cards or tied sets of cards) of representative titles between two neighbouring ranks of standard titles; and that they could place one or more ranks of representative titles above the topmost standard title or below the lowest standard title. In this way, some common basis for the ranking and the scoring of the representative titles could be secured.

Before employing this procedure it was, however, necessary to subject it to practical trial, in particular to ascertain whether the selection of the common set of 20 standard occupations was in any degree critical. To this end we carried out a small pilot study in which the procedure was the reverse of that proposed for the main study, in that we used a single set of 20 dummy 'representative' titles which did not vary from respondent to respondent, but employed two sets (A and B) of standard occupations, each constructed to span the whole range of social standing in a fairly regular fashion. In accordance with our intentions for the main study, the respondent was asked to grade the standard occupation titles first and then to interpolate the dummy representative titles. In this way we were able to try out the procedures of the main inquiry and, by standardizing one and the same set of representative titles in terms of two standard sets, to determine whether the choice of standard set made any difference to the assessment or scoring of the representative occupations.

This pilot study was conducted in the London area by five interviewers obtained through a commercial fieldwork agency, Mary Agar Field Service Ltd., and trained by the authors.* Since sampling was not of any moment, each interviewer was asked to obtain a representative quota sample of ten respondents according to the usual procedures of market research. Fifty envelopes were made up with interview material, 25 containing set A standard occupations and 25 containing set B standard occupations. Assignment of the two sets of envelopes was random, the envelopes were numbered, and interviewers were given blocks

* We wish to acknowledge the most helpful collaboration of Mrs. Mary Agar and her staff.

of consecutively numbered envelopes and instructed to use them in strict number order. This ensured that respondents were randomized between the two sets of standard occupations.

Interviewers were instructed to record the final ranking of all occupations exactly as for the main study (see p. 51), and the procedure by which scores were assigned to the dummy representative occupations was exactly the same as that used to assign scores to the real representative occupations in the main study. The procedure involves first of all taking the grades of the standard occupations, closing them up to eliminate the gaps which appear when the grades of the representative occupations are removed, and centring and standardizing them. A dummy representative occupation which was tied with a standard occupation was given the same centred and standarized score as the latter. The remaining representative occupations were scored in terms of their neighbouring standard occupations following specific rules (for full details, see chapter 4, p. 54).

The assessment and scoring of the representative occupations were thus in all respects identical with the procedures used in the main inquiry. For purposes of analysis, however, the distribution of scores of dummy representative occupations for each respondent was centred and standardized. (This was not done in the main inquiry because the purpose of the scoring procedure was to render commensurate gradings of sets of representative occupations which differed from respondent to respondent.) Because every respondent graded one and the same set of 'representative' occupations, we can apply to the centred and standarized gradings an analysis of variance procedure similar to that used in Appendix A. In addition to Respondents and Occupations we have a third source of variance which is the difference between grading and scoring representative titles in the context of set A standard titles and grading and scoring the same representative titles in the context of set B standard titles.

The analysis is set out in Table B1. In the estimation of variance components it is assumed that all three terms are random. Because the model is completely random it is possible to read off two correlation coefficients very simply from the variance components. The correlation between the average respondent who graded set A standard occupations and the average respondent who graded set B standard occupations is 0·6308. The average correlation between two respondents, both of whom graded the same set of standard titles is 0·6308 + 0·0061 = 0·6369. The difference between the two correlations is so small as to be negligible. We conclude, therefore, that choice of set of standard occupations as a framework for the grading and scoring of representative occupations is not critical.

As well as allowing us to assess the differential effect of the two sets of standard occupations, the London inquiry also gives us an opportunity to assess the absolute value of reliability coefficients obtained from gradings carried out within the framework of a standard set. The coefficient 0·63 is an indication of the reliability with which representative occupations are graded by a single respondent. It is however, inflated by two factors. The first is that the sample of respondents is a quota sample and therefore likely to produce a greater degree of reliability than the random sample of the main inquiry. The other is that the

TABLE B1

Analysis of data from the London pilot inquiry to study the effect of differing sets of standard occupation titles on the scores assigned to dummy representative titles. The data are those analysed in Table B1 but here they have not been centred and standardized. All terms are assumed to be random

Source	d.f.	Sum of squares	Mean square	Variance component
Occupations	19	609·0664	32·0561	0·6308
Occupations × Sets	19	9·7862	0·5151	0·0061
Occupations × Respondents × Sets	912	331·1474	0·3631	0·3631
Sum	950	950·0000	—	1·0000

TABLE B2

Analysis of data from the London pilot inquiry to study the effect of differing sets of standard occupations on the scores assigned to representative titles. The data are those analysed in Table B1 but here they have not been centred and standardized. All terms are assumed to be random

Source	d.f.	Sum of squares	Mean square	Variance component
Sets	1	0·0223	0·0223	–
Occupations	19	711·6034	37·4528	0·7384
Occupations × Sets	19	10·1212	0·5327	0·0048
Respondents within Sets	48	38·1130	0·7940	0·0190
Occupations × Respondents within Sets	912	377·0795	0·4135	0·4135
Sum	999	1136·9394	–	1·1757

analysis has centred and standarized the distributions of scores of representative occupations, thus removing two sources of possible error which were present in the main study.

The analysis of variance was repeated without the preliminary centring and standardization of the distribution of dummy representative occupations, that is, with the latter in the form in which they were scored in the main inquiry. The analysis is shown in Table B2.* If each variance component is divided by the sum of the variance components in order to reduce it to the same proportionate terms as the components in Table B1, the correspondence between the two analyses is very close. The extra term in Table B2, which represents differences among the means of respondents, accounts for 2 per cent of the variance, and the reliability coefficient is lower by an equivalent amount: 0·61 instead of 0·63. We concluded therefore that the reliability of the assessment and scoring procedure employed in the main inquiry was likely to be of the order of 0·6, possibly with some further reduction because the sampling is random rather than quota.

The figure $r_{tt} = 0·6$ represents the reliability of assessments provided by a single respondent. It may be compared with the coefficient $r_d = 0·56$ in Table A3 which represents the extent of agreement between two respondents grading occupations on the same dimension in the Oxford four-dimensional study, and with the coefficient $r_{tt} = 0·46$ which represents the average level of agreement between two different respondents grading occupations on the criterion of 'social standing'. The indirect process of assigning scores by interpolation of representative titles into a distribution of standard titles appears to produce a higher level of reliability than the less structured but more direct procedures of the Oxford inquiry. The differences may of course be due in some part to differences in sampling procedure or to differences between the kinds of interviewer employed (students in the case of the Oxford inquiry and market research interviewers in the case of the London pilot study).

The usual formula for the reliability of the mean of assessments of an occupation by k respondents is

$$\frac{kr_{tt}}{kr_{tt} + (1 - r_{tt})} .$$

From this it can be calculated that assessments with a reliability in excess of 0·9 may be achieved by averaging gradings over no more than k = 10 respondents when the individual respondent has a reliability in the region of $r_{tt} = 0·6$. The actual coefficients obtained may of course drop below 0·9 in certain circumstances, for example, in the grading of relatively unspecific or unfamiliar occupations. The standard error of assessment may also not be uniform along the whole length of the occupational distribution.

* It is not easy to see why the mean square for Sets should be smaller than any other mean square by a factor of 20. Presumably the constraint which brings this about is related to the fact that Sets is not only a classification of respondents but also a scoring procedure for assigning values of the dependent variable in the analysis.

APPENDIX C

THE NATIONAL INQUIRY—DETAILS OF THE SAMPLE

The sample was a self-weighted random sample from 30 parliamentary constituencies in England and Wales, with two polling districts in each constituency.

In order to select 30 constituencies, the geographical area of England and Wales was divided into the standard regions and conurbations as defined by the Registrar General's *Statistical Review* (OPCS, 1969). These divisions were made so that highly urban areas (the conurbations) and less urban areas (the standard regions minus the conurbations) might have a better chance of being properly represented in the sample. Both the conurbations and the standard regions (minus the conurbations that fell within them) were then listed by the parliamentary constituencies that they contained. In the few cases in which a parliamentary constituency straddled a boundary, the constituency was assigned to that area in which the greater part of its electorate appeared to lie.

When these lists had been prepared, the total number of electors in each region and conurbation was calculated using a summary of the 1971 Register of Electors information. Then, each area total was divided by the total number of electors in England and Wales, and this quotient was in turn multiplied by 30 to establish the number of constituencies that should be selected in each area in order to represent it in proportion to its population.

After this calculation had been completed, several constituencies were shifted to different areas and two categories were entirely merged with others. This was done so that in each area the final figure representing the number of constituencies to be selected might more nearly approach an integer. As far as possible, like was kept with like, e.g. urban areas were kept with urban areas. The final figures achieved for each area were the following:

1.	Tyneside	0·78
2.	The North	1·30
3.	Yorkshire and Humberside	1·90
4.	West Yorkshire	1·10
5.	South-east Lancashire	2·06
6.	The North-west	2·05
7.	East Midlands	2·07
8.	West Midlands (conurbation)	1·82
9.	West Midlands (region)	1·28
10.	East Anglia	1·02
11.	South-east	
	a. borough constituencies	1·96
	b. county constituencies	3·99
12.	Greater London	
	a. North	1·82

175

	b. South-west	1·11
	c. South-east	1·83
13.	South-west	2·30
14.	Wales	1·70

The method by which the requisite number of constituencies was selected varied slightly from area to area. From the areas for which only one constituency was to be chosen, i.e. Tyneside, the North, West Yorkshire, the West Midlands region, and East Anglia, the parliamentary constituencies were listed and a cumulative sub-total of their electorate was taken. With the use of a random number table, a number between 1 and the total number of electors in the area was found and the constituency whose interval contained this number was chosen.

For Yorkshire and Humberside, the North-west, the East Midlands, and the South-west, the constituencies were first divided into county constituencies and borough constituencies. This was done as another way of separating the areas which were more likely to be highly urban—the borough constituencies—from those which were less likely to be highly urban—the county constituencies. In consequence, each type had a better chance of being properly represented in the sample. Subsequently, the county constituencies were listed from lowest to highest in order of the percentage of the vote that went to Labour in 1970. Then, the borough constituencies were listed in order from highest to lowest.* The constituencies were listed from lowest to highest, then from highest to lowest, to ensure that if a low Labour vote county constituency was selected, a high Labour vote constituency would probably be the other one selected (whether it was a county or borough constituency depended on what proportion of the people in an area were in county and borough constituencies). Similarly, if a high Labour vote county constituency was chosen, this method of ordering made it likely that a low Labour vote borough constituency would be the second one chosen. After the constituencies had been ordered in this manner, cumulative sub-totals of the electorate in the constituencies were taken. The total was then divided by 2, and a random number between 1 and this quotient was picked, yielding the first constituency to be chosen. The second constituency was chosen by adding the quotient to the random number.

A similar procedure was followed for Wales. Industrial Welsh constituencies were listed from lowest to highest by percentage of Labour vote; the remainder of Wales was listed from highest to lowest, and then the same procedure as outlined above was followed. For the West Midlands conurbation, the constituencies were divided into Birmingham and others, listing the others from lowest to highest and Birmingham from highest to lowest. Again, the same procedure as before was then employed.

* As the sample was to be drawn on the new parliamentary boundaries, the percentages of Labour vote for constituencies in which there were no or only minor boundary changes were taken from the 1970 election figures. For constituencies in which major boundary changes were involved, the percentages were Dr. D. E. Butler's best guess of what the percentage would have been if the new boundaries had been in effect in 1970.

For South-east Lancashire, the constituencies were simply listed from lowest to highest by percentage of Labour vote, since the urban/non-urban basis of division did not exist. A random number between 1 and one half of the electorate was chosen to pick one constituency and the other was found by subtracting the random number from the total. This procedure was followed in order to ensure that if a constituency with a relatively low Labour vote was chosen, a constituency with a relatively high one would also be chosen, and *vice versa.*

The South-east was divided into borough constituencies (from which two were selected) and county constituencies (from which four were selected). In both cases, they were ordered by alternately placing the constituency with the lowest Labour vote at the top of the list and the one with the next lowest at the bottom, working into the middle. A random number was chosen between 1 and a half of the electorate (for the boroughs) and 1 and a fourth (for the county constituencies) Then this number was added to the interval of one-half and one-fourth respectively.

Greater London was split into 3 geographical areas—the North, the South-west, and the South-east. In each area the constituencies were ordered from lowest to highest percentage of Labour vote and in the North and South-east the same procedure as that used for South-east Lancashire was employed. For the South-west, only one constituency was required, so one random number made the selection.

After the 30 constituencies had been selected, the next step was to choose 2 polling districts from each. This was done by listing all the polling districts in the constituency (using the 1971 electoral registers) and taking cumulative sub-totals. A random number between one and one-half of the total selected the first polling district, and the second was chosen by subtracting the random number from the total. Consequently, the more people there were in a polling district, the greater its chance of being selected.

It was decided to draw a sample of 1,600 names for the 620 interviews required. We were working on the expectation of a refusal rate of up to 35 per cent. The extra names were to compensate for the facts (a) that the sample was to be drawn from the 1971 rather than the 1972 Registers, thereby inflating the numbers that would be lost because of death, demolition, and moving,* and (b) that we would lose some people because they were outside the age limits of the sample (20 to 64 years inclusive).

Since the figures listed on pp. 175f were not whole numbers, the number of interviews in each constituency was adjusted to compensate for this fact. Consequently, 620 (the number of interviews) was divided by 30 (the number of constituencies) and then multiplied by the figures on pp. 175f for each constituency to establish how many interviews should be completed in each. Similarly, 1,600 (the number of names to be drawn) wad divided by 30 and multiplied by the appropriate figure to ascertain how many names should be drawn for each constituency. After both set of figures had been rounded to even integers, they were

* In fact, we lost one polling district—V— from the Ardwick constituency in Manchester. We drew another polling district—P—to supplement the addresses that were still standing in V. A number between 1 and the total number of electors in Ardwick was used to select this additional polling district.

divided by 2 (polling districts) to yield the number of interviews and the names per polling district. The sampling interval in each polling district was the number of electors in it divided by the number of names. A random start was taken, and then every nth (the sampling interval) name. Young voters were excluded (they were outside our age limits); service voters and voters living in institutions (defined as an address with 10 or more people) were also excluded.

Each interviewer was issued with 50 per cent more addresses than interviews to be completed. The remaining names were held by the area supervisors to be issued if needed by giving out two additional addresses for every interview lacking for a sample point. The sampling interval was the number of remaining addresses divided by the number of addresses needed. The interviewers were unaware of the additional names held by the area supervisors.

In addition to the names taken from the electoral registers the sample, included some persons who were not listed in the 1971 Register for the chosen addresses. At each address, the interviewer listed any persons between the ages of 20 and 64 inclusive who were not on the 1971 electoral register for that address. (She had been supplied with a complete list of names on the register for the address.) She then numbered these persons from eldest to youngest and consulted the selection table (Kish's boxes) on the contact sheet for that address. In order to use Kish's (1965) method, it is necessary to ensure that contact sheets are employed in a determinate order. To achieve this each interviewer was supplied with as many contact sheets as she had addresses. She was instructed to use her contact sheets from the top (the interviewers were instructed at the briefings to number their contact sheets in order, so that if they were dropped, the order could be reconstituted). The contact sheets were issued in a rotating order of selection tables. The interviewer was to attempt to gain an interview with the person selected by the table.

A discussion of the response rate obtained from the scale is contained in chapter 4, pp. 51–54. Table C1 provides the detailed analysis on which this discussion is based.

TABLE C1

Details of response to the main grading inquiry

Address issued to interviewer but not required to fulfil quota	64
Person contacted but outside the age limits 20—64	180
Address demolished	33
not found	5
empty	19
Person dead	22
moved	165
not known at address	4
away	35
No reply	33
Person unfit for interviewing (ill, handicapped, unable to speak English, etc.)	22
Refusal	145
Appointment made but not kept	14
Interview schedule rejected (and reused) because of interviewer error	2
Interviews achieved	620*
	1,363

* This total includes schedules for two eighteen-year-old interviewees. We did not deem these errors a matter of sufficient moment to justify their removal and the reuse of the schedules.

APPENDIX D

THE NATIONAL INQUIRY—INSTRUCTIONS TO INTERVIEWERS

Materials

1. For each interview there is a numbered envelope containing a schedule and a *corresponding* set of 40 cards (20 blue, 20 white), each bearing the name of one of the 40 occupations on the schedule. The occupations on the blue cards are the same for every informant; but no two sets of white cards have exactly the same occupations on them.

2. There are also six pink cards, each bearing the name of an occupation. These are *specimen* cards, are so labelled, and are for use as specimen cards *only*, as indicated below. Keep the pink cards and the instruction sheets from your sample kits—there are none in the envelopes.

3. A *large* table or similar piece of furniture, clear of objects is a highly desirable feature of the interview situation. If no such piece of furniture is available, then the best alternative is to use a clear space of floor. At all events, try to avoid having the informant perform the grading task in unduly limited space.

4. Authentication card from Nuffield College, Oxford

Relating evelopes to informants

1. The envelopes containing the interview materials each have a serial number. They are to be administered to persons on your name sheet *in strict number order,* using the lowest numbered first.

2. If an interview is broken off, cross out anything you have written on the schedule and *reuse* if for the next informant.

3. The following is a suggested self-introduction: 'I am working on behalf of Nuffield College, Oxford, on a study of occupational change. We are interested in people's views on the social standing of different occupations, and we would very much like you to take part in the study.'

Filling out the contact sheets

1. Starred electors

(i) You should *always* interview the starred persons on your list of names and addresses if they are between 20 and 64 years old and are living at the address on the list.

(ii) For each starred name, you should fill out one of the white contact sheets. At the top, enter the sampling point number and the name, serial number and address of the starred person, all of which can be found on the typed address list. In addition, fill in your name and interviewer number.

(iii) In the squared box beneath 'I.Starred Person', record the dates, times and results of all your calls.

(iv) Please enter the results of calls in the following way:

> interview
> too young—age . . .
> too old—age . . .
> house empty
> house demolished
> moved
> too ill
> dead
> away on holiday
> refusal.

In the case of refusals, please give full details: reasons given, circumstances, who refused, etc.

(v) After administering the grading task to an informant, you should mention that we sometimes like to talk to people again, a fortnight or so later. Ask if there would be any suitable dates and times when we might call back after a fortnight. Enter this information on the white contact sheet in the lower right-hand corner.

2. Selected non-electors

(i) We are also interested in interviewing certain people who are not on the list. You should list the ages of all males and females aged 20 to 64 who are living at the same address as the starred person, but who are *not* on your typed list. Ask 'Are there any people living in this household other than [read list] who are aged between 20 and 64?'

(ii) If there are none, tick that box on the contact sheet. If it is impossible to fill out this section because of an irrevocable refusal, tick the appropriate box.

(iii) If there are some people aged 20 to 64 in the household not on the list, number them beginning with the eldest and ending with the youngest. (Ask 'who is the eldest?', 'who is next?', and so on.) Consult the selection table on the contact sheet to find the person you are to interview. Circle that number and place a tick by that person. Then try to arrange an interview and record the results of calls in the usual way. Find out suitable times to call back in a fortnight's time as you did for the starred electors, but be sure to indicate clearly to whom the dates and times apply if there are two interviews recorded on one contact sheet, i.e. the starred person and a selected non-elector.

3. Repeat interviews

For the envelope marked 'R', you should use the blue rather than the white contact sheets, filling in the information at the top and entering the name of the person to be reinterviewed and the result of calls in the same way as for the first interview.

Administering the grading task (take your time and say the instructions slowly)

1. Show the informant the six pink cards, placing them at random on the table.

2. Say to the informant—'I am going to give you 20 cards like these. On each one is the name of an occupation. I'm going to ask you to arrange the occupations according to what you think is their *social standing*. I want you to put the cards in a column so that the occupation which *you think* has the highest social standing is at the top, with the rest following in order until you have the occupation with the lowest social standing at the very bottom. Or, alternatively, you can start at the bottom and work up. If you think any two or more occupations have the same social standing, just put their cards side by side. You can "tie" as many cards like this as you like. [*Demonstrate with the pink cards.*] Try to think of the occupations generally and not of particular people in them ... Can we try it on these six cards [i.e. the pink ones]? Which occupation do you think has the highest social standing ...?' It is desirable that the interviewer should learn this instruction by heart before starting on the interviews.

3. Go through the grading of the six pink cards, prompting if necessary: 'and the next highest ...?' etc. When this is done, pick up the six pink cards and put them away: 'Good, that was just a trial run.'

4. Take the 20 *blue* cards from the envelope and spread them out before the informant. Say: 'Now, I want you to do the same thing with these 20 cards that we have just done together—to arrange the occupations according to what you think is their social standing. Take as much time as you need, and change your mind as you want to as you go along. Have you any questions? Should I go over anything again?'

5. When the informant has graded the 20 cards, say: 'Now, are you quite happy with that [do not pause here] because I wouldn't want you to alter that order later on?' When the informant appears definitely settled on the grading, widen out the spaces between the cards in the column—but *without disturbing the order of the grading*—so that there is somewhat more than two card widths between each card or set of 'tied' cards and the next.

6. Produce the 20 white cards, and say to the informant: 'Now here are another 20 cards with occupations on them just as before. I want you to arrange them also according to their social standing by fitting them into this column of 20 blue cards that you have already made. Let me show you what I mean with these pink cards'. Take the six pink specimen cards and demonstrate the various possibilities as you are saying them—*viz*.: 'You can put white cards *in-between* blue cards—one, two, three or as many as you like; or you can "tie" white cards with blue cards—again as many as you like; or you can put white cards *above* your highest blue card or *below* your lowest blue card. In other words, just fit the white cards in with the blue ones wherever you think the occupations should

go according to their social standing. Is that all clear? Do you think you have the idea?' If so, or when, put away the six pink cards and hand the informant the 20 white cards. Again, it is desirable that this instruction should be learned by heart. Take care that the blue cards are not accidentally knocked out of order when the white cards are being inserted.

7. When the informant has graded all 20 cards, ask: 'You have already said that you are happy with the order of the blue cards, are you quite happy with the white ones? If so, I'll go ahead and record the order.' Record the informant's gradings of *all 40* occupations on the chart provided on the interview schedule. (At this stage the blue/white difference is of no significance.) The occupation(s) on the top card or set of cards should be recorded as 1 on the schedule. The occupation(s) on the next card or set of cards should be recorded as 2 on the schedule. And so on. At the end, check that the number you record for the lowest ranking card or cards is equal to the total number of ranks that the informant has used. (This will, of course, be 40 or less, how much less depending on the number of ties.)

8. Pick up all the cards and replace them in the envelope with the schedule.

9. *Some miscellaneous points*
(i) If the informant asks what is meant by 'social standing' tell him that he should just think of what this means to him and grade the occupations accordingly.

(ii) If the informant seems in any doubt at all, make clear that what you are interested in is what *he* thinks the social standing of an occupation *is*—not what he thinks *others* think it is, or what he thinks it *ought* to be.

(iii) If an informant says that he is unfamiliar with an occupation given on a card, encourage him to judge its social standing according to what he thinks the occupation might be. *But do not attempt to explain to him what the occupation is.* We would much prefer a guess to a refusal to include an occupation in the grading. If, however, an informant does refuse, record a dash against the occupation on the chart rather than writing nothing at all.

(iv) We would much prefer that informants did *not* change the order of the blue cards once they start fitting in the white ones. This is why we ask you specifically to check that they are happy with their grading (point 5 above). But if anyone insists on making such changes, write a note indicating how the initial order of the blue cards differed from the final order that you have recorded on the interview schedule. All indications of changes must be made in terms of the names of occupations, *not* in terms of ranks or grades, e.g. 'bank clerk was originally immediately below salesman', or 'engineer and computer programmer have been interchanged'. If in any doubt, it is safest to write down the whole of the *initial* order before the informant makes his changes (as well, of course, as the final order recorded in the usual way).

(v) If there is a discrepancy between the schedules and the cards, use a piece of paper to make a new card to replace an incorrect or missing card. The occupations on the schedule are correct and if a discrepancy occurs it is the cards which are wrong.

Completing the first sheet of the interview schedule

1. The questions should be straightforward except for occupation. In this respect the instructions given in the attached note generally apply. Where a man is unemployed or retired, record his *last* occupation. If he has never had an occupation, note the circumstances—e.g. is still a student, is disabled. In the case of women informants:

—if married or widowed, record husband's occupation (or last occupation)
—if single or divorced, record informant's own occupation, if any; or if unemployed or retired, last occupation; or if never employed, note circumstances.

2. Tick the box indicating whose occupation you are recording.

Repeat interviews

1. We shall be reinterviewing some of the informants after two weeks have elapsed. The materials and procedures for the second interview for a particular informant are exactly the same as those for the first interview, except that the first sheet of the schedule is shorter.

2. Separate envelopes containing the materials for the second interview will be issued, each marked with an 'R'. The instructions for administering the second task are the same as those for administering the first. Thus, at the start of the repeat interview, you should tell the informant that you want him or her to do exactly the same thing as on the first occasion; but you should add: 'I don't want you to try to think back to what you did last time—just rank the occupations according to how you feel about their social standing now.' You then proceed to run through the instructions as before.

3. If the informant asks, you can tell him that the occupations are exactly the same as last time. If the informant asks the reason for being asked to do the whole thing over again, give an explanation on the following lines: 'We think that some people may have rather different ideas from the first time, while others may say much the same—but there is no question of right or wrong about it, so don't try to think back. I just want you to order the occupations according to how you feel now.'

Notes on the preceding instructions to interviewers

'Non-electors' (persons residing in the household but not on the electoral register for the address) who were between the ages of 20 and 64 inclusive were sampled using the selection-table procedure described by Kish in *Survey Sampling*

(1965). The selection tables were printed on the contact sheets issued to the interviewers. Eight different tables were employed but four of these were used with twice the frequency of the others. Twelve piles of contact sheets were made (eight of them being pairs of duplicates, the other four containing the less frequent selection tables) and sheets were taken off the piles in unbroken cycles of twelve, each interviewer being given as many sheets as addresses (the number of addresses assigned was 50 per cent greater than the number of schedules to be completed). On receiving the addresses for a polling district, the interviewer numbered the contact sheets in the order in which they had been taken from the original piles and she was instructed to make her calls in the order of the address list and to use the contact sheets in their number order.

Interviewers were asked to record on the contact sheet for every address a suitable time to reinterview the listed informant at that address two weeks after his or her initial interview (and also to obtain a convenient reinterview time for the selected 'non-elector', if any). They were therefore aware that some inform-ants would be reinterviewed but they were not told that the informants to be reinterviewed would in fact be those whose schedule numbers were divisible by eight without remainder. Special contact sheets and duplicate interview materials for the reinterviews were issued by area supervisors to interviewers. The super-visors saw to it that no informant was interviewed twice by the same interviewer.

REFERENCES

ASCH, S.E., BLACK, H., and HERTZMAN, M. (1938). Studies in the principles of judgements and attitudes. *J. of Psychology*, 5, 219–51.

ATKINSON, J. (1968). *A Handbook for interviewers*. H.M.S.O., London.

BARBER, B. (1957). *Social stratification*. Harcourt and Brace & Co., New York.

BECHHOFER, F. (1969). Occupations. In M. Stacey (ed.), *Comparability in social research*. British Sociological Association and Social Science Research Council, London. Heinemann, London.

BLAU, P.M. (1957). Occupational bias and mobility. *Amer. Sociol. Rev.* 22, 392–9.

BURT, C. (1955). Test reliability estimated by analysis of variance. *Brit. J. Statist Psychol.* 8, 103–18.

DEPARTMENT OF EMPLOYMENT (1972). *Classification of occupations and directory of occupational titles*. H.M.S.O., London.

DUNCAN, O.D. (1961). A socioeconomic index for all occupations. In A.J. Reiss (ed.), *Occupations and social status*. Free Press of Glencoe, New York.

DUNCAN, O.D., and ARTIS, J.W. (1951). *Social stratification in a Pennsylvania rural community*. Pennsylvania State College: Agricultural Experiment Station Bulletin 543.

FISHER, R.A. (1963). *Statistical methods for research workers* (13th edn.). Oliver and Boyd, Edinburgh.

GALTUNG, J. (1967). *Theory and methods of social research*. Allen and Unwin, London.

GERSTL, J., and COHEN, L.K. (1964). Dissensus, situs and egocentrism in occupational ranking. *Brit. J. Sociol.* 15, 254–61.

GLASS, D.V. (ed.) (1954). *Social mobility in Britain*. Routledge and Kegan Paul, London.

GOLDTHORPE, J.H. (1960). Status and conflict in industry: a critique of two aspects of the personnel policy of the National Coal Board. Cyclostyled, N.C.B. Library, Hobart House, London.

GOLDTHORPE, J.H., LOCKWOOD, D., BECHHOFER, F., and PLATT, J. (1968). *The affluent worker: industrial attitudes and behaviour*. Cambridge University Press.

GOLDTHORPE, J.H., LOCKWOOD, D., BECHHOFER, F., and PLATT, J. (1969) *The affluent worker in the class structure*. Cambridge University Press.

GOLDTHORPE, J.H., and HOPE, K. (1972). Occupational grading and occupational prestige. In K. Hope (ed.), *The analysis of social mobility: methods and approaches*. Clarendon Press, Oxford.

GRAY, P., and GEE, F.A. (1972). *A quality check on the 1966 ten per cent sample census of England and Wales*. H.M.S.O., London.

HALL, J., and JONES, D.C. (1950). The social grading of occupations. *Brit. J. Sociol.* 1, 31–55.

HODGE, R.W., TREIMAN, D.J., and ROSSI, P. (1966). A comparative study of occupational prestige. In R. Bendix and S.M. Lipset (eds.), *Class, status and power* (2nd edn.). Free Press of Glencoe, New York.

HOPE, K. (1969). The study of hostility in the temperaments of spouses: definitions and methods. *Brit. J. Math. Statist. Psychol.* 22, 67–95.

HOPE, K. (ed.) (1972). *Oxford studies in social mobility*. Working Papers Vol. I. *The analysis of social mobility: methods and approaches*. Clarendon Press, Oxford

HUTCHINSON, B. (1969). Social status and inter-generational social mobility in Dublin. The Economic and Social Research Institute, Paper no. 48, Dublin.

HYMAN, H. (1954). The value systems of different classes. In R. Bendix and S.M. Lipset (eds.), *Class, status and power* (1st. edn.). Routledge and Kegan Paul, London.

INTERNATIONAL LABOUR OFFICE (1968). *International standard classification of occupations.* I.L.O., Geneva.

KISH, L. (1965). *Survey sampling.* Wiley, New York.

KOHN, M. (1969). *Class and conformity: a study in values.* Dorsey Press, Homewood, Illinois.

LAUMANN, E.O., and GUTTMAN, L. (1966). The relative associational contiguity of occupations in an urban setting. *Amer. Sociol. Rev.* 31, 169–78.

MACDONALD, K.I. (1972). MDSCAL and distances between socio-economic groups. In K. Hope (ed.), *The analysis of social mobility: methods and approaches.* Clarendon Press, Oxford.

MACDONALD, K.I. (1974). The Hall-Jones scale: a note on the interpretation of the main British prestige coding. In J.M. Ridge (ed.), *Mobility in Britain reconsidered.* Clarendon Press, Oxford.

MAHMOUD, A.F. (1955). Test reliability in terms of factor theory. *Brit. J. Statist. Psychol.* 8, 119–35.

MANN, M. (1970). The social cohesion of liberal democracy. *Amer. Sociol. Rev.* 35, 423–39.

MORRIS, R.T., and MURPHY, R.J. (1959). The situs dimension in occupational structure. *Amer. Sociol. Rev.* 24, 231–9.

MOSER, C.A., and HALL, J. (1954). The social grading of occupations. In D.V. Glass (ed.), *Social mobility in Britain.* Routledge and Kegan Paul, London.

NATIONAL INSTITUTE OF INDUSTRIAL PSYCHOLOGY (NIIP) (1951). *The Foreman.* Staples, London.

NATIONAL INSTITUTE OF INDUSTRIAL PSYSCHOLOGY (NIIP) (1957). *The place of the foreman in management.* Staples, London.

OFFICE OF POPULATION CENSUSES AND SURVEYS (OPCS) (1968). *Standard industrial classification.* H.M.S.O., London.

OFFICE OF POPULATION CENSUSES AND SURVEYS (OPCS) (1969). *Registrar General's statistical review of England and Wales.* H.M.S.O., London.

OFFICE OF POPULATION CENSUSES AND SURVEYS (OPCS) (1970). *Classification of occupations, 1970.* H.M.S.O., London.

OPPENHEIM, A.N. (1966). *Questionnaire design and measurement.* Heinemann, London.

OSGOOD, C.E., and STAGNER, R. (1941). Analysis of a prestige frame of reference by a gradient technique. *J. of Appl. Psychol.* 25, 275–90.

PILLINER, A.E.G. (1965). The application of analysis of variance in psychometric experimentation. Unpublished Ph.D. thesis, University of Edinburgh.

REISS, A.J. (1961). *Occupations and social status.* Free Press of Glencoe, New York.

RIDGE, J.M. (ed.) (1974). *Oxford studies in social mobility.* Working Papers Vol. II *Mobility in Britain reconsidered.* Clarendon Press, Oxford.

ROSSI, P.H., and INKELES, A. (1957). Multidimensional ratings of occupations. *Sociometry,* 20, 234–51.

SVALASTOGA, K. (1959). *Prestige, class and mobility.* Gyldendal, Copenhagen.

TAFT, R. (1953). The social grading of occupations in Australia. *Brit. J. Sociol.* 4, 181–8.

TAUBMAN, P. (1973). Occupational coding. *Annals of Economic and Social Measurement,* 2, 71–87.

THOMPSON, F.M.L. (1963). *English landed society in the nineteenth century.* Routledge and Kegan Paul, London.
TIRYAKIAN, E. (1958). The prestige evaluation of occupations in an under-developed country: the Phillipines. *Amer. J. Sociol.* **63**, 390–9.
URMSON, J.O. (1950). On grading. *Mind*, **59**, 145–69.
WEBB, E.J., CAMPBELL, D.T., SCHWARTZ, R.D., and SECHREST, L. (1966). *Unobtrusive measures: nonreactive research in the social sciences*. Rand McNally, Chicago.
WILLMOTT, P. (1963). *The evolution of a community.* Routledge and Kegan Paul, London.